D1188797

INSIGHT INTO HELPING
SURVIVORS OF CHILDHOOD

SEXUAL ABUSE

7-99.

WAVERLEY ABBEY INSIGHT SERIES

INSIGHT INTO HELPING SURVIVORS OF CHILDHOOD
SEXUAL ABUSE

Heather Churchill and Wendy Bray

CWR

Copyright © 2012 CWR

Published 2012 by CWR, Waverley Abbey House, Waverley Lane, Farnham, Surrey GU9 8EP, UK. Registered Charity No. 294387. Registered Limited Company No. 1990308.

The right of Heather Churchill and Wendy Bray to be identified as the authors of this work have been asserted by them in accordance with the Copyright, Designs and Patents Act 1988, sections 77 and 78.

For list of National Distributors visit www.cwr.org.uk/distributors

Unless otherwise indicated, all Scripture references are from the Holy Bible: New International Version (NIV), copyright © 1973, 1978, 1984 by the International Bible Society.

Concept development, editing, design and production by CWR

Printed in Finland by Bookwell

ISBN: 978-1-85345-692-3

WAVERLEY ABBEY
INSIGHT SERIES

The *Waverley Abbey Insight Series* has been developed in response to the great need to help people understand and face some key issues that many of us struggle with today. CWR's ministry spans teaching, training and publishing, and this series draws on all of these areas of ministry.

Sourced from material first presented over Insight Days by CWR at their base, Waverley Abbey House, presenters and authors have worked in close co-operation to bring this series together, offering clear insight, teaching and help on a broad range of subjects and issues. Bringing biblical understanding and godly insight, these books are written both for those who help others and those who face these issues themselves.

CONTENTS

FOREWORD

The need to help those who have been sexually abused in childhood is arguably greater today than at any time in history. Jesus saved His sternest rebuke for child offenders, 'If anyone causes one of these little ones to stumble, it would be better for them to have a large millstone hung around their neck and to be drowned in the depths of the sea.' It is reasonable to assume that He alone knew the long-term damage and consequences of child abuse. Evidence suggests that child abuse, at the hands of a family member or a person known to the child is as rife in church circles, including Evangelical ones, as it is in the wider community.

Congratulations Heather and Wendy for providing the Church with such a timely resource. This book is a must read for the Christian who wants to take action on behalf of those who have been wounded and hurt as a result of sexual abuse in childhood. The authors share wise insights and practical professional guidance relevant not just to counsellors but also those who are willing to share the journey in other roles, as trusted friends and pastoral carers.

Practical and professional, and scripturally based, this book provides powerful and perceptive insights about how best to minister to these precious survivors of abuse – people made in God's image whom He has 'crowned with glory and honour', of immeasurable worth and value, both to Him and to us. It contains specialised advice and information that counsellors need and is accessible to non-professionals too. I particularly appreciated the conclusion of each chapter; some of the most poignant and perceptive prayers I have ever read.

Supporting someone through the aftermath of abuse is never a quick fix, it is a long haul. Most of the work of recovery is dealing with the emotional wreckage caused and requires painstaking rebuilding of that crucial sense of self-worth, security and significance. This superb resource is for anyone with a heart to see healing and restoration for the survivors of childhood sexual abuse.

I believe that caring for those sexually abused in childhood – who suffer such emotional, psychological and spiritual isolation, shame, pain and sorrow – is a remarkable ministry. I am convinced that this book, so full of grace and truth, will be an invaluable encouragement and guide to all who find themselves walking alongside and offering comfort, care, healing and hope. In the same breath as Jesus issues His stern warning to child abusers He says this: 'For I tell you that in heaven their angels are always in the presence of my heavenly father.'

I believe there is a great rejoicing amongst the angels in heaven for the healing and hope brought by putting into practice the principles outlined in this brilliant book whose aim is to transform survivors into thrivers!

Lyndon Bowring
Executive Chairman, CARE

INTRODUCTION

In 1999 I was a CWR student on the Diploma in Counselling course run at London School of Theology (then London Bible College), listening to the devotional teaching of Selwyn Hughes and counselling training delivered by other CWR tutors. During that year, I received a phone call from a client who hinted that she had a 'difficult problem' and wondered whether I would see her. The 'difficult problem' turned out to be that her father had repeatedly sexually abused her throughout her childhood and that now, in adult life, she was finding it difficult to come to terms with what had happened. This was the first of many, many clients I have seen over the years, who have had this difficult story of sexual abuse to tell.

I have been humbled by the dignity, courage and great bravery my clients have shown in facing the pain of what happened in their childhood. This book is dedicated to them all. My prayer is that the readers of this book will be able to help and understand others who have been sexually abused in early life, and that ultimately those who have been abused themselves will find a measure of healing and be able to know and experience God's love in a deeper way.

Heather Churchill

CHAPTER 1

HELPING THOSE WHO HAVE BEEN SEXUALLY ABUSED IN CHILDHOOD: WHERE TO BEGIN

Our concern begins with two simple questions: How might we best accompany one another on life's journeys? And how might we best help those whose pain, as a result of their particular journey, is almost unimaginable to us?

Those of us who wish to follow in the footsteps of Jesus know that we are called to offer Christlike compassion; compassion which involves a willingness to share the deepest pain and to take action on behalf of those who are voiceless or powerless. Sharing the journey of someone who has been sexually abused may require us to do both.

The purpose of this book is to help those who are called upon to share that journey as accompaniers to listen and respond well, in addition to understanding that *each has a unique role to play.* Counsellors, pastoral assistants, trusted friends or clergy can all offer vital support, but we will see that the means by which they do this might be different.

This book will not answer every question or address every situation, but our hope is that it will impart some understanding of what it is to be sexually abused and the challenges faced in shaping life in the aftermath of that abuse. We will also consider some practical guidelines for support and the accompaniment process.

In this brief introductory chapter, we will attempt to clarify how we can begin to offer that support and accompaniment by identifying the needs of those who are abused and suggesting some working definitions. We will also look at the varying contexts in which an experience of sexual abuse might be shared and identify the needs both of the abused person and the listener or counsellor (accompanier). In other words, we are asking: 'What are we being asked to do in our accompaniment of someone who has been sexually abused and how can we prepare to do it as best we can?'

APPROACHING THE JOURNEY

The first person we inevitably see as we approach this difficult journey is the person who has been abused. As we draw close to them it is vital that we see them first and foremost for who they are: someone made in God's image whose worth is far beyond our imagining and who is loved and valued by Him accordingly. Any kind of abuse attempts to mar that image, to reduce worth and dignity and to shatter self-esteem through pain, shame and powerlessness. Part of our task on the accompanying journey will be to restore a correct understanding of that image and, with it, a sense of self-worth and value. In addition, it is worth noting that, in childhood, an abused child is rarely in a position to exercise control. Therefore, as we come alongside the survivor, it is vital we ensure that the abused person feels that *they* retain control; that we are not 'doing something' to them or prompting them to disclose information when they are not ready. Otherwise their sense of being controlled will occur again. They *must* be assured that they are in the 'driving seat' at all times.

The second person we see as we approach the start of the journey is our own self: the one who is called upon or challenged to be an accompanier, perhaps reluctantly, often fearfully. Yet we do want to help. So we will move beyond our reticence, our sense of inadequacy and fear and, recognising the need for self-awareness, begin to listen and look for what is needed and how we might best respond. For this reason, it is important to differentiate between the different roles of the accompaniers.

DIFFERENT ROLES

If we are a friend, layperson or clergy member, we will very likely be the first to hear the disclosure of abuse. Our role is to listen and support, never to promise total confidentiality and, quite early on in the process, usually, to say: 'This might be important enough to merit us seeking professional help.' Using the word 'us' gives clear indication that we are not giving up, not abandoning the one who has been abused nor expecting them to go on alone. Instead, our role is to help by signposting the way ahead in helping them to find a professional counsellor who has the experience and expertise to help, and *to stay with them as they do so*, in a clearly defined supporting role.

We need to understand that, in most cases, the work ahead is skilled and difficult: for the survivor, the friend and the counsellor, as well as others involved. A concerned friend, for example, should not attempt to tackle some of the physical and emotional effects of abuse that this book addresses – flashbacks, nightmares, self-harm, depression, dissociation – any more than they might attempt to carry out major surgery. First Aid theory tells us that a little knowledge is a dangerous thing and that our first responsibility is to assess whether there is any further danger to the one we are seeking to help. None of us would want to be that danger personally.

Because of the necessity for clear and distinct roles, we will more specifically refer to the survivors of sexual abuse we are accompanying as 'clients', assuming that many of us reading this book will be trained counsellors and that our relationship will be one that is beyond a friendship or pastoral role. This is *not* to exclude those of us whose vital role is as clergy, friend or supporter – since what is here will help and inform us too – but to first and foremost protect the vulnerable people we are seeking to help, to retain boundaries, to ensure accountability and to give the utmost care to everyone involved.

IDENTIFYING A SURVIVOR'S NEEDS
a) Being heard

As well as feeling safe and in control of the journey they are undertaking, what many clients of sexual abuse want more than anything is to be heard (and heard, and heard again): to know that what they are saying in word, action, and in any way they can communicate, is acknowledged, believed and held by us as we hear their story. Research[1] clearly indicates that most of those abused in childhood will keep their experience to themselves for some time, often not disclosing it even in adult life. There are several reasons why children (and, for that matter, adults too) are reluctant to disclose. One is that children who have been abused often tend to respond with self-blame and self-doubt. This in itself makes it difficult to report abuse. A further reason is the fear of what might happen when they disclose the fact that they have been abused – what will be the consequences of such disclosure? Many fear they will not be believed or that they personally will be the cause of a family breakdown.

The words we use in talking about the experience of those who have been abused are therefore very important and we will discuss in detail the types of responses which are helpful and unhelpful in Chapter 4. For now, it is worth recognising at this early stage the devastating effects of sexual abuse on a person, both in childhood and in later adult life.

b) Being validated as more than a victim

Nevertheless, however devastating the abuse and however it has clouded their life, those who have been abused will not (usually) want that experience to define or dictate their life. While the abuse was happening, they were a victim. Now that they have lived beyond what is a terrible ordeal, they are very much a *survivor*. (However, for some the word 'survivor' smacks of struggle and just 'keeping your head above water', so they may prefer a word closer to *thriver*.) Recognising the fact of that word change – allowing the client to choose how they see themselves – and the onward movement it indicates, recognises the strength and resilience used to come this far. Whilst the pain a survivor still feels is not to be underestimated, the character, determination and strength that have brought them thus far are considerable.

Acknowledging this offers the survivor some hope for the future as they find ways to integrate what has happened to them (and sometimes what has directly or indirectly happened to others as a result) into the life they live today and the plans they make for tomorrow. Survivors, or thrivers, might only be able to do this through acknowledging every aspect of their pain and suffering: physical, emotional, sexual and social. Moving forward will mean that they will relive, acknowledge and continue to hold painful memories of betrayal, bewilderment and physical and emotional harm in ways that will help them to live beyond the abuse in a realistic and healthy way.

c) Being helped as an individual with unique and distinct circumstances

Like any journey of recovery, the path ahead is unpredictable. It's essential to go where and with what the survivor (the client) wants and is ready for. For example, full disclosure could take years – or may not ever be fully achieved. So this is a journey that will involve moving forward, retracing steps, struggling in dark valleys, noticing sudden breaks in the clouds and periods both of being rooted to the spot and wandering round in circles. Whatever the nature of the journey, every element is necessary in order to make genuine progress along a difficult road.

The needs of a survivor (as client) are complex, varied and dependent upon a number of factors. These include: who the abuser or perpetrator was; the context and timescale involved; the nature of the abuse; and the consequences both for them as a victim and survivor and for others.

The Reverend Dr Marie M. Fortune has identified seven elements to the process embedded in this journey:[2]

- The opportunity to share the story of abuse
- For someone to hear and believe that story and acknowledge its consequences
- For that someone to show compassion and a willingness to accompany – rather than just trying to 'fix it'
- For the abused individual and others who may be vulnerable to be protected from further harm where possible
- For the community to hold the perpetrator to account in some way
- To see an act of restitution as far as possible
- To know unambiguous vindication

The final outcome of this process or journey and the number of these elements that each survivor (or client) needs to experience to make progress is a difficult issue that raises many questions. What is the journey working towards? Is it a case of a client 'coming to terms with'; 'moving on'; reaching 'healing' or 'wholeness'? Or is it all four in indistinct stages? Fortune's list clearly highlights just how important elements of justice and accountability are as part of the process. For some, moving forward may be painful but bearable, yet reaching the journey's end and any form of 'wholeness' or recovery can seem improbable, if not impossible. Many survivors will live with a metaphorical image of what the abuse has done and how it has left them. They may find it helpful to think about the abuse having 'got them' in its grip. So aiming for a 'You've got it now' instead of 'It's got you' offers hope, without suggesting or guaranteeing that the experience can ever be deleted from their lives, or that they need to 'arrive'. For this reason, at some point close to the beginning of their journey, they could be helped to frame exactly what they are hoping for, or believe they might achieve, in sharing their experience and working through it. They might even surprise themselves in exceeding those expectations.

THE CONTEXT FOR HELP AND SUPPORT

The journey forward for survivors of sexual abuse is deeply complex, widely emotional and highly individual. How that journey or process begins and continues (and with whom) will usually largely depend on where, and with whom, the client feels safe and fully heard. To begin with, this may be in the context of a trusted friendship, through conversation with a member of the clergy or pastoral team, or in a direct counselling relationship – often where the abuse isn't mentioned until several sessions into a programme.

Laypeople, pastoral personnel and clergy within churches will often be challenged by the very complex needs of those who are survivors of abuse and should be wary of two extremes: the first of thinking that they 'can cope' when disclosure happens; and the second of making a referral to a skilled counsellor immediately. If referral is suggested as a first response, in some cases the client may take their story no further, having used every ounce of emotional energy in sharing it the first time. Staying alongside a client, continuing to listen and offering constancy and compassion are first and foremost the most helpful things to be done. As we explained earlier, friends, laypeople or clergy may well need to enlist the support of a specialist counsellor outside and beyond the pastoral relationship. It is therefore essential to clarify the boundaries of perceived roles and confidentiality at an early stage.

CONFIDENTIALITY

Boundaries of confidentiality between friend or layperson and survivor, counsellor and client – and what they mean in practice – may need to be spelt out.

Whatever our role, we can never promise total confidentiality because:

- Anyone involved is likely to need 'supervision' of some kind, be it professional or informal.

In addition, the client could:

- Become suicidal
- Threaten to put someone else's life at risk
- Disclose that there are specific children in danger (which would result in both a moral and legal obligation to disclose abuse to the relevant authorities).

All of the above would necessitate action on our part and the involvement of at least a third party. However, for survivors of abuse, trust is a massive issue since the abuse itself represented a huge betrayal and breakdown of trust. For this reason, whatever role we play (friend, helper, clergy or counsellor) we must take great care to maintain confidentiality and to seek advice from a trusted professional if we are ever unsure whether we need to break confidentiality.

TAKING CARE

We are probably all aware of the the 'Oxygen Mask Principle'. Traditionally, when aircraft passengers are shown how to use their oxygen masks in the case of an emergency, they are instructed to put their own masks on first, *before* trying to help those who are younger or less able to fix their own masks in place. Those of us who care, counsel and listen are not always good at generalising and applying that advice! But it is essential that we put safeguards in place.

When we find ourselves listening, often unprepared or for the first time, to details of sexual abuse we cannot help but be disturbed, shocked or traumatised. It is essential that as counsellors we are given professional supervision, and that as pastoral carers, clergy or laypeople we seek wise support, so that we can address the issues raised – not least issues of self-awareness – in order to protect both ourselves and the abused person. Counselling clients can be a very emotional experience and can provoke numerous personal issues, even for those experienced in this area. It is easy, in our compassion, to over-identify and become over-involved in the client's situation.

Wilson and Thomas[3] caution:

> As the therapist gets pulled into the patient's inner world of traumatisation and the magnetic force of his or her trauma story and personal state of injury, the stark reality and devastating extent of the patient's trauma experience may become so real that it seems like the therapist's own experience. Realities and boundaries may blur, creating states of confusion. This phenomenon has been variously labelled vicarious traumatisation, empathic distress, traumatic counter-transference and affective overload.

Self-awareness, self-care and preparedness include observing the guidelines set out opposite.

For friends, clergy and laypeople, we should:

1. **Clarify the limits and purpose of confidentiality** in a conversation as outlined above.
2. **Have a trusted person or partner** with whom we can share, in confidence, our own responses to what we have heard.
3. **Make ourselves aware** of other sources of varied support which might be needed and available for the person we are seeking to help – especially professional counselling.
4. **Follow the guidelines 4–5 below.**

For counsellors:
1. **Supervision is vital** – as much to offload some of the detail of what has been heard as for reasons of shared professional advice and support.
2. **Set caseload limits** – as a professional counsellor choose to limit helping clients who have suffered the trauma of sexual abuse to 50% of a case load.
3. **Clarify the limits of confidentiality.** As soon as we become aware that someone wants to confide in us, assure them that we will maintain confidentiality, but with the following exceptions: 'I will need professional supervision'; 'If I felt that you were a danger to yourself or to others, or that there was a child protection issue, I would need to let someone else know.' In stating this, it is important to stress that these measures are for their safety and ours.
4. **Maintain boundaries of possibility.** Focus on what we *can* do – while remaining realistic about what we cannot do.
5. **Express our own anger** at what we have heard. Each of us has a chosen way: making bread; bouncing a ball; shouting in the middle of a field; playing the piano fast and furiously; kick-boxing ...

6. **Build in a healthy balance of life and play.** Do something different; indulge in some self-pampering; focus on what is good, true and healthy; enjoy friends and family, fun and laughter.

7. **Find a way to 'close the file'.** Find other ways to offload or 'close the file' at the end of a session. Write notes or a summary; pray; go through a particular 'shutting off' routine, for example visualise putting the 'file' in a box and shutting it away in a cupboard on a high shelf.

8. **Keep our own relationship with God healthy.** Maintain our Bible reading and prayer life, and participate in the life of our worshipping community as a high priority.

Fiona, an experienced counsellor, was working with Jane, who, in their third session, had disclosed particularly traumatic sexual abuse at the hands of her husband. Although Fiona had worked with clients of sexual abuse before, she had not encountered it within marriage and she found Jane's story particularly disturbing and difficult to deal with. Thinking that she should be able to cope and that the complexities of Jane's situation were too great, Fiona did not share Jane's situation within group supervision. It was only when Fiona became quite depressed and anxious, almost fearing her sessions with Jane, that she realised that she could not bear the burden alone. Fiona arranged for individual specialist supervision with another counsellor with greater experience of sexual abuse.

TAKING NOTES

In a professional setting, we may wish to keep appropriate records or notes of our work with clients. It is essential, due to the nature and potential criminality of the abuse, that we take care. When notes are made, counsellors should take into account their client's rights and the counsellor's responsibilities under Data Protection legislation. In addition, it should be borne in mind that there is the possibility that the notes may be read by the client, by the police and by legal counsel, or even read out in public in a Court of Law. Therefore, as with all client notes, great care should be taken to ensure that the records are accurate, respectful towards the client and factual, avoiding the inclusion of any hunches or personal thoughts the counsellor may have. It is also helpful to get into the habit of prefacing relevant statements with 'the client reported'. In addition, we need to remember that however carefully we may record our notes, we might be accused of influence, which could potentially jeopardise the possibility of any future prosecution attempt.

AWARENESS OF BROADER CONTEXTS

There are, of course, broader social and legal contexts to abuse, to its consequences and to its disclosure. Sexual abuse is, at the very least, a moral crime and one which has a devastating impact on the person. It is a crime that is committed in private with implications that are potentially public and punishable by law. But it is also a crime committed in secret, something which makes it particularly perilous and painful for a client to pursue to the courts.

The legalities are complicated, so we must be clear about them. The UK Government offers this advice:

The key factors in deciding whether or not to share ... (such) information (i.e. refer to the relevant authorities) are necessity and proportionality (i.e. whether the proposed sharing is likely to make an effective contribution to the public interest if sharing information overrides the interest in maintaining confidentiality). In making the decision you must weigh up what might happen if the information is shared against what might happen if it is not.[4]

Whatever path is taken, pastoral care (eg in a church setting) should always be separated, as much as is possible, both from professional specialist counselling and from the carrying out of an investigation into the abuse. It is important to separate the legal, clinical and pastoral aspects of support, whilst allowing one to inform the other as is necessary and helpful. The decision to seek justice and report abuse to the police will usually rest in the hands of the client (unless there is a legal obligation for the helper/counsellor to disclose). However, it is always helpful to thoroughly explore the potential ramifications of this decision with the client in order to help them have as full an understanding and awareness of the consequences of this action as possible. Sadly, the majority of those who are abused find little or no redress within the criminal justice system – especially when the abuse took place years ago or in situations where the perpetrator is no longer alive.

We cannot reiterate enough that the overriding factor in supporting those who are survivors of sexual abuse is that we listen to their story and acknowledge their pain; and that we listen, or facilitate that listening, for as long as it is needed. To be heard is to know dignity restored: we believe it is what Jesus would have done.

Having explored our initial approaches, we will move on in Chapter 2 to examine how sexual abuse might be defined and understood.

REFLECTION

Jesus was often to be found listening to the stories of those who lived painful lives – pain which they often felt isolated them from others, for a variety of reasons.

Take time to read one or two of the following Gospel accounts of these conversations. What are the hallmarks of Jesus' encounters? How did He begin each relationship? What can you learn from them?

(NB: Our focus is on the attitude of Jesus, not the individual circumstances of those to whom He ministered. It is not appropriate to draw specific parallels with the circumstances or character of those who have been abused.)

Luke 8:42b–48: The woman who touched Jesus' cloak

Mark 1:40–42: The man with leprosy

Mark 2:1–5: The paralysed man brought to Jesus by his friends

John 4:7–26: The Samaritan woman at the well

As you reflect on the beginning of this journey of accompaniment – or the possibility of it – how do you feel about being asked to follow in these particular footsteps of Jesus?

About being His listening ear? His voice for those who have no voice?

Inadequate? Fearful? Angry, maybe?

It may help to imagine yourself standing alongside Jesus as He listens, speaks and acts in these Gospel accounts; to learn from His attitude, His listening, His gesture.

Imagine that as His interaction draws to a close, He turns to you and says, 'And now, over to you ...' What will you say? What will you do?

PRAYER

Father of compassion,

Jesus, the Son, who knows what it is to be wounded and abused,

Holy Spirit, who counsels, heals and reconciles,

commission me by Your power and with Your compassion

to do Your work among those for whom Your heart breaks.

Make me aware of my limitations, my weaknesses, my vulnerabilities.

May each of us allow You to mend broken hearts and bind wounds and bring freedom.

Enable me to share, with great wisdom, these first steps of a painful journey with another,

both of us encouraged – even unknowingly – by Your love and hope.

Amen.

CHAPTER 2

DEFINING SEXUAL ABUSE: AN OVERVIEW OF WHAT AND WHO

DEFINITION AND CONTEXT: BLURRED BOUNDARIES

To define sexual abuse is, inevitably, to narrow and exclude. But we do need a working definition. We might begin with what sexual abuse *isn't*, but even here boundaries can be blurred: instead, we may need to look for characteristics rather than activity.

Sexual abuse, like any abuse (physical, emotional or spiritual), often has a primary characteristic of power rather than, as many would assume, sexual activity. Sexual abuse is essentially about *power differentiation*. In other words, if we take a young person as an example of the person being abused, the abuse is carried out in a context where the young person is unable to make a decision as to whether to engage in sexual activity due to their relative lack of knowledge and power. Having established this key characteristic, we can make a clear distinction between 'normal' sexual behaviour (such as that indulged in by curious children playing 'doctors and nurses') and the point at which that curiosity might cross a boundary into power-centred sexual gratification (that is, when something is done to someone/asked of someone without their consent or despite their anxiety or bewilderment). In other words, what is 'beyond the boundary' is behaviour which is not invited or welcomed and which is not shared consensually through mutual agreement and understanding.

When considering childhood sexual abuse, we might work with one or both of the following definitions:

Firstly, and more simply, the American National Center on Child Abuse and Neglect 1978[1] suggests that *child* sexual abuse may be defined as:

Contacts or interactions between a child and an adult, when the child is being used for the sexual stimulation of the perpetrator or another person when the perpetrator or another person is in a position of power or control over the victim.

Or the more specific guidelines from the UK Government's *Working Together to Safeguard Children*:

... forcing or enticing a child or young person to take part in sexual activities, not necessarily involving a high level of violence, whether or not the child is aware of what is happening. The activities may involve physical contact, including assault by penetration (for example rape or oral sex) or non-penetrative acts such as masturbation, kissing, rubbing and touching inside of clothing. They may also include non-contact activities, such as involving children in looking at, or in the production of, sexual images, watching sexual activities, encouraging children to behave in sexually inappropriate ways, or grooming a child in preparation for abuse (including via the internet).[2]

Despite the cultural landscape, a sexual act with a young person under the age of sixteen remains a criminal act, added to which some consensual acts initiated by an older person with a person under the age of eighteen – especially where they are seen as a 'trusted' adult or to be exploiting a position of power – may also be considered to be criminal.

The Government definition of child sexual abuse is broad and helpful, especially in the use of the phrase *'whether or not the child is aware of what is happening'*, as many perpetrators will use the supposed innocence of their victim in defence. This definition also draws attention to the growing problem of internet-based sexual crime. However, as we will discover in the next section, we must remember that the vast majority of cases of sexual abuse are by persons known to the victim.

Sheila was abused as a child of eight when shown pornographic films by an older cousin. She was unaware of what she was witnessing, except that what she saw was disturbing and frightening. She largely blocked out her memories and only some years later, when she accidentally witnessed a clip of a pornographic film, did she remember what she had suffered and begin to suffer flashbacks.

Andrea was raped repeatedly by her grandfather at the age of five, having been told that 'Every little girl does this', while Douglas suffered dozens of incidences of inappropriate touching by a church minister who befriended him as a lonely only child.

All of these are experiences of sexual abuse, each resulting in considerable trauma and the need for long-term counselling and support.

Abuse is also framed by cultural practices, such as ritual abuse, satanic worship and FGM (Female Genital Mutilation) in certain cultures and by forced marriage. The growing and often insidious practice of child exploitation and people trafficking[3] for purposes of prostitution also frequently involves organised sexual abuse.[4]

PERPETRATORS: EXPLODING MYTHS

Our focus here is on the survivor of abuse and for that reason we need to generalise regarding the perpetrators. Rather than try to pinpoint likely abusers, it may be more helpful to explode myths.

It is most certainly a myth that sexual abuse only occurs in certain subgroups of society, eg amongst poor or isolated families. Evidence shows that abusers come from every social, ethnic and employment background and are found amongst every age group. It is striking, however, that one third of all sexual offences against children are committed by other children and young people, especially adolescents.[5] In these cases, it is defined as abuse because of the power differentiation: for example, a fifteen-year-old abusing a vulnerable nine-year-old.

Neither do adults who have been sexually abused always go on to abuse: there is clear evidence that abusers are more likely to have experienced physical and emotional abuse, including bullying, in childhood. Nor are abusers exclusively male. Studies show that up to 20% of suspected paedophiles are women.[6]

In 2009, two women were sent to prison for child sexual abuse, charged as accomplices of a man: they pleaded guilty to sexual assault on very young children and to swapping indecent images. One of the women worked as a nursery worker in a respected day-care nursery in Plymouth and, as such, had easy access to very young babies and toddlers. The case horrified the community and left parents traumatised, not knowing whether their own children had suffered abuse. Many commentators made specific reference to the fact that two out of the three perpetrators had been women, overturning the solid belief that sexual abuse of young children was confined to men.

As Christians we might like to believe that abuse doesn't happen in Christian families or churches. That mistaken belief is refuted by press coverage to the contrary, as well as by the caseloads of Christian counsellors.

Finally, despite the widespread perception that children are abused mostly by strangers, research shows that, in the main, sexual abuse is perpetrated by someone who is known to the child. The person might be a member of the family, a family friend or someone with whom the child comes into regular contact.[7]

In other words, in most cases the person who sexually abuses a child is an adult who is known by the child and who has access to them by virtue of his/her authority: a relative, family friend, neighbour, teacher, club supervisor, priest or community worker.

In 2005, the charity telephone helpline, Childline, received 11,976 calls from children reporting sexual abuse. Of those, 59% reported that they had been sexually abused by a family member, and 35% reported that they had been abused by someone known to them and the family. Only 5% reported being abused by a stranger.[8] Therein lies the abuse of power and trust, since the abuse usually occurs in the context of a child's relationship with an older person from whom the child had every right to expect care and protection.

Although news stories reporting the whereabouts of paedophiles may cause hysteria, these statistics suggest that the hysteria is largely misplaced. While we should be concerned and vigilant in the face of such revelations, we should also remember that the vast majority of sexual abuse occurs within the family or known close community, rather than within the wider one. Consequently, it can happen anywhere, at any time, to anyone.

Julia, a church leader's wife, rang a telephone helpline for church leaders and their families, run by a national charity. She told the listener that she had made several attempts to do so as she was desperately pulled between loyalty to her husband and fear for her daughters. Her husband, a well-loved and respected church leader, had sexually abused her eldest daughter, Anna, while Julia had been away visiting her elderly mother. On Julia's return, Anna had appeared distant. Eventually, with a great deal of anxiety and tearful struggle, Anna told Julia that her father had got drunk and had started touching her inappropriately. He had also said that she wasn't ready for sex yet but 'soon would be'. Anna – and Julia – were both helped to begin the difficult process of gaining professional help and support outside the context of the church. The fallout was devastating, but both mother and daughter were supported as they recognised the necessity of full disclosure.

NSPCC research indicates that one in four girls and one in six boys will be abused at some time before their eighteenth birthday.[9] Such abuse is not primarily an isolated event. Home Office Research suggests that 66% of victims experienced repeated abuse over five years or more.[10] Abuse was a single event in only 6% of cases.

Research conducted in the United States suggests that 15 to 30% of females and 5 to 10% of males report some exposure to childhood sexual abuse. Estimates of severe forms of childhood sexual abuse, involving full penetration, range from 5 to 10% of all children.[11]

In familiar terms we could say that as we stand as part of a congregation on a Sunday morning, or sit in a busy pizza restaurant amidst a crowd of one hundred or so, there is a likelihood that we will be alongside approximately twenty people who have been sexually abused, in some way, in childhood. Contrary to popular belief, sexual abuse is not a rare occurrence for a few; it is a painful reality for too many.

HOW DO WE KNOW THAT SOMEONE HAS BEEN ABUSED?

We don't. Victims and clients of abuse are indistinguishable in society, in our neighbourhoods and in our worshipping communities. Counsellors report that clients often don't disclose abuse in an initial assessment session. Since they have carried their 'secret' for many years, great bravery and assurance of trust are needed to disclose that secret to someone else. We may often pick up on 'hints', odd remarks or parts of stories dropped into the counselling dialogue, or in pastoral or general conversation. These represent a 'testing' of safe ground: 'Will this person be shocked?'; 'Can I tell them more?'; 'Will I be believed?'; 'Am I safe in this place?' It takes considerable skill to pick up the tiny knotted threads of those hints and offer – or signpost – a safe place in which to unravel the resulting tangle of secrecy and pain.

CHALLENGES AND CONTROVERSY

THE FALSE MEMORY SYNDROME CONTROVERSY

Counsellors who work with survivors of abuse are sometimes faced with issues raised by the False Memory Syndrome controversy.[12] As the title of the syndrome suggests, it is a controversial subject. There are two sides to consider:

1. Inability to remember

On the one hand, there is considerable evidence that it is possible to forget episodes of abuse: the age of the victim at the time of the abuse is the strongest determinant for amnesia. Children under the age of six are least likely to recall abuse immediately, often only recalling the trauma in adult life. Research suggests[13] that the younger a child is when experiencing abuse, the less cognitive ability they have to encode memories. This is often a self-preservation mechanism – in other words: a child, in order to cope with something impossibly difficult, will blot it out. As a result of this way of coping, there is evidence[14] that a person can have a sudden recall of previously suppressed memories when exposed to a relevant trigger.

2. Suggestibility

On the other hand, memory is not a neat science or an exact process. When we try to remember, we continually engage in the process of trying to make sense of situations (to smooth out the gaps in our personal narrative), using both reason and imagination.

It must be acknowledged that there are published accounts which have included instances where clients have recovered 'false memories' following suggestions from their therapist.[15] Perhaps this is not surprising, because as traumatic memories unravel, and following intrusive suggestions by others, a client might find that false memories surface in order to help them make some sense of the situation. The likelihood of this happening is also closely linked to the client's level of openness to proposals made by others (suggestibility).

IMPLICATIONS FOR COUNSELLORS

It is of great importance that as counsellors we take enormous care not to 'suggest', in any way, what we think may or may not have happened to those we are listening to. This may happen because we are trying to make the retelling less painful for our client, or because we want to make progress. Suggesting anything is a clear example of us taking over the 'steering wheel' of disclosure. The client should always be in the driving seat. Instead, as counsellors, we must make space and time to allow memories to surface.

Another useful analogy is that we may wait patiently under the tree for the fruit to fall, but we should never shake the tree. (Although we can pray for a helpful gust of wind in the right direction!) Those clients who share memories without any leading questions or helpful 'prodding' are less likely to be vulnerable to suggestibility. They will have more ownership of their disclosure and be less likely to doubt their own experience, which will enable them to move forward.

It can be very difficult for very young children who have been abused to make any sense of what has happened to them, or to find ways to verbalise their experience, hence the common use of toys or dolls in therapy. Yet children will, of course, be particularly anxious to please or to 'give the right answer', especially when they have learned to behave in a 'pleasing' way in an abusive relationship. Often they will search the face of the one asking the questions, watching for any clues that they are on the right track and are doing what they think is required of them. We must take great care.

In the next chapter, we will move on to look at the symptoms and effects of sexual abuse in young children, teenagers and surviving adults and consider how our understanding might help us to help them.

REFLECTION
Read Genesis 1:26–27.

Much of the work we do with those who have been abused is about restoring the image of God in the abused person. Not the image we see or God sees, but the self-image held by the one whose view of self has been so damaged and marred by their experience.

Ask yourself ...

How does the nature of abuse – the loss of power; the having things 'done to'; the possible sense of guilt; the imposition of secrecy – mar that image?

How does abuse take away freedom and significance?

As you reflect on these questions, ask God how you might begin to restore 'His image' in the life of the one you are accompanying.

How might you make this restoration the backdrop to your work?

PRAYER

Creator God,

You have made us in Your image, to reflect Your glory and to draw us into close relationship with You.

As I walk with this person, whom You love so much, enable me to find ways for us to 're-etch' that image, line by line, as together we begin to bring some small element of restoration and freedom into a damaged life.

Amen.

CHAPTER 3

THE SYMPTOMS AND EFFECTS OF CHILDHOOD SEXUAL ABUSE

In this chapter we will look at what we might recognise as *symptoms* of sexual abuse, consider what the *effects* of abuse are for children, teenagers and adults, and set both in the context of some psychological research. In other words, we will try to explain what to look for in terms of the emotional and behavioural impact of abuse and how we might understand both in order to help clients.

THE RESPONSE AND UNDERSTANDING OF VICTIMS AND SURVIVORS

Historically, the effects of childhood sexual abuse have been minimised. As late as the 1940s, social scientists researching the incidence and effects of incest in families did so by considering the *social* context of the abuse, failing to recognise the emotional and sexual impact.[1] However, during the last thirty years, mental health professionals have increasingly recognised that sexual abuse in childhood can have a significant impact on a child's development and their subsequent mental health in adult life.[2]

The response to, and impact of, sexual abuse varies widely from person to person. Some survivors may seem able to process what has happened and move on. Others will struggle with the resulting pain and trauma for many years. Neither response is 'right' or 'wrong'; and, accordingly, there can be no 'hierarchy'[3] of abuse. Nevertheless, all survivors will live in varying degrees of shadow of that abuse, whether they have been able to disclose the experience to others or not. Some will bury their memories, consciously or unconsciously, re-experiencing the trauma of what has happened at a much later date. Others will wake each morning to the impact of what they have experienced and will find ways (often harmful) of coping with that impact: perhaps through drinking, drugs or episodes of self-harm. A sense of powerlessness and lack of self-esteem are common.

Failing to make sense of what has happened to them, children will often perpetuate the sense of helplessness they felt in an abusive situation. They may even become eager to please in order to increase a sense of self-worth, thereby unknowingly making themselves more vulnerable to further abuse in the process. What complicates the child's response is often an inability to understand what constitutes 'normal' behaviour from an older person. Confusion can also result when the abuse produces some level of involuntary sexual arousal or pleasure. (We will deal with this in more detail in Chapter Six.)

Amy joined Sue's reception class at the age of just five. She was a pretty and lively child, often dressed in fashionable clothes which Sue felt were styled a little too much like those of a teenager. Bright and capable, if attention-seeking in class, Amy was a joy to teach. However, her behaviour changed utterly when a male member of staff was nearby. Becoming animated, Amy would 'drape' herself around the male teacher, expecting attention. Kind but firm rebuttal did little to change Amy's behaviour, which only became more overtly sexual. After interviews with Amy's parents, the school found it necessary to involve the Child Protection Team as there was the suggestion that Amy had possibly been abused by one of her parents' male friends. Amy had not learnt what was normal or acceptable, even in the context of family life.

SYMPTOMS OF CHILDHOOD SEXUAL ABUSE: CAUTION REQUIRED

Before we begin, it is important to remind ourselves that symptoms which might point to sexual abuse may also have a different cause entirely. With caution in mind then, common symptoms or signals of childhood sexual abuse might be:

- Changes in school performance, decreased interest, difficulty in concentrating
- Medical complaints such as anal and vaginal infections, urinary tract infections
- Sexualised behaviour – inappropriate sexual behaviour for the age of the child

- Regression – bed wetting, thumb sucking etc
- Sleep disturbance – sleepwalking, nightmares

SYMPTOMS OF SEXUAL ABUSE IN TEENAGERS

These may be the same or similar to those of younger children, but might also include:

- An avoidance of sports – especially where they were previously enjoyed
- Shame about puberty, periods etc
- A negative body image. This is, of course, common amongst teenagers but may take a particularly worrying form or be linked to ...
- The development of eating disorders – anorexia, bulimia
- A drop in standard of academic work/behaviour in school
- Sexual problems – promiscuity, prostitution
- Impulsive behaviour – self-harm, substance abuse, drinking, truanting, stealing

EFFECTS OF CHILDHOOD SEXUAL ABUSE ON CHILDREN

We have already mentioned that every survivor of childhood sexual abuse (whether child, teenager or adult) is unique in their response to the abuse they have suffered. The abuse may be very similar in nature to that suffered by someone else – even taking place within the same family – yet two siblings may be affected very differently. However, there are common effects. Sexual abuse by a trusted adult can impact the development of the child's sense of self-esteem and sense of self.

Firstly, the child can begin to doubt who they are and what they are 'for'. This may be in addition to the doubts they hold about the nature of the relationship they had understood before the abuse took place, and the safety and security of the environment they had trusted. In other words, abuse threatens the most basic needs for attachment and emotional security with others – something a child should be able to depend upon.

To help us understand these specific effects, it may be helpful to draw on Attachment Theory, formulated by John Bowlby, and his explanation of the formation of a child's sense of self and self-esteem.[4]

Bowlby argued that an infant's emotional attachment/ relationship to their primary care-givers has a cognitive component. In other words, in childhood we form mental representations which result in beliefs about self and the interpersonal world. Bowlby referred to this as an 'internal working model'; a model of the way a child views themselves, others and their environment (see Fig. 1).

(FIG. 1) BOWLBY'S INTERNAL WORKING MODEL

If the primary care-giver is:
- harsh
- cruel
- abusive
- unreliable
- distant
- unpredictable

Then a person's internal view of the world includes:
A sense of self as:
unworthy | guilty | responsible | invalid | unwanted

A sense of the primary carer as:
threatening | anxiety-provoking | unsafe

A sense of the world as:
dangerous | painful

But if the care-giver is:
- reliable
- loving
- available
- responsive
- consistent
- close

Then the person's internal view of the world includes:
A sense of self as:
worthy | valued | cared for

A sense of the primary carer as:
dependable | safe | connected | nurturing

A sense of the world as:
safe | hopeful

So, when children experience their care-givers as safe and responsive to their needs (both physical and emotional) the concept of self that is formed is one of worth and value. Alternatively, where there are problems with either the physical closeness or emotional response of the care-givers (for example, when a child is sexually abused by her father) then it is likely that this child will develop an understanding of self that is unworthy, invalid, guilty and in some way to blame for the abuse.

It is important to add that the child was *not* to blame, and never should be blamed, for the sexual abuse. However, children who have been abused are likely to feel and believe that they *are* to blame. (We will deal with how to help a survivor with this misplaced self-blame in Chapter Five.)

These cognitive structures might be more easily understood as a 'filing cabinet' of stored information in the brain; information that significantly influences the way a child, and in later life the adult, interprets information. These cognitive components can become so ingrained in childhood that they generally operate automatically, outside of conscious awareness in later life.

THE EFFECTS OF SEXUAL ABUSE ON INFANTS AND TODDLERS

One of the effects of abuse on infants and toddlers can be seen to be a marked disruption of the attachment process leading to what is called 'disorganised-insecure attachment'. During the 1970s, psychologist Mary Ainsworth developed Bowlby's work on Attachment Theory with her 'Strange Situation' study. This involved observing children between the ages of twelve and eighteen months as they responded to a situation in which they were systematically and briefly left alone and with a stranger and then reunited with both the stranger and with their mother.[5] Ainsworth concluded that there were three major styles of attachment: secure attachment, ambivalent-insecure attachment and avoidant-insecure attachment. (The study makes interesting reading in depth.) Although not entirely without criticism, numerous later studies have supported and developed her conclusions. What is helpful for us is that researchers Main and Solomon (1986)[6] later added a fourth attachment style known as 'disorganised-insecure attachment'. They identified a particular reaction in small children who had been severely emotionally and/or sexually abused. In disorganised/disorientated attachment the child appears dazed, disorientated, almost 'trance like'. Main identified that in this fourth 'attachment style' the primary attachment figures were observed as both a safe haven and a source of danger, resulting in the disorientation.

Further research[7] has shown that if children have been sexually abused (mainly by close members of the family) they tend to demonstrate disorganised attachment histories. They will exhibit a sense of helplessness and a mixture of a need and longing to approach and connect with others, coupled with a fear of what might happen when they become close to others. Consequently, they develop a need to avoid. Mental representations also become distorted. When this happens, a child may develop different coping strategies in his bewilderment. Firstly, he may become very compliant and eager to please to minimise the stress he is feeling, or he may demonstrate symptoms of hypervigilance, remaining 'on the lookout': alert, jumpy, irritable and hyperactive or in a constant state of fear and arousal.

Kelly, at age seven, was physically very small for her age and both a charming and challenging child. She was seated close to her teacher in class, both to encourage her to remain sitting down in order to concentrate on schoolwork and to enable her teacher to keep her as calm as possible. Kelly was constantly on the move: her behaviour alternated between being ultra compliant and eager to please to freezing when asked to do something. Whenever possible she would flit around the classroom in a dream world, then would suddenly watch the door or look out of the window in a state of anxiety.

Kelly began to refuse to undress for P.E. She would run, trembling, into the arms of her teacher every morning, and was reluctant to leave school at the end of the day, often hiding under tables or in cupboards. Bruises were discovered on her arms and legs, and in the course of investigation it became clear that Kelly was being sexually abused by her mother's boyfriend.

THE EFFECT OF ABUSE ON BRAIN FUNCTION

Research suggests that trauma in childhood can impact brain development and maturation. In her book, *Why Love Matters*[8], Sue Gerhardt explains how experiencing love in early infancy is essential to brain development. On the same basis, childhood trauma, such as abuse, can have a profound impact on the development of the brain. This can, in turn, impact future wellbeing and mental health in adult life.

PSEUDO MATURITY

An abused child may sometimes assume a caring role with regard to other siblings – often in an attempt to protect them from also being abused. Their sense of self may then develop in the context of only being worthy if they care for others.

DIFFICULTY IN REGULATING EMOTIONS

Abused children often find it difficult to regulate emotions. They might wrongly learn that anger is unacceptable, or that tears are not allowed, and find it hard to use their emotions to communicate appropriately. Tantrums and noncompliance can result, with corresponding difficulties in relating to other people, especially their peers. This means that the child is often isolated in the playground. Isolation is a key to being abused, making the child an easy target. As no one is looking out for them, they are viewed by a paedophile as 'easy prey' – and isolation perpetuates their vulnerability.

It is not surprising then that children who have been abused can develop a number of affective disorders. For example, abused children demonstrate higher rates of depression than children who have not been abused. Indeed, research also indicates that adults who have suffered sexual abuse in childhood are 2.4 times more likely to suffer mental health difficulties in adult life than those who have not been abused.[9]

ATTRIBUTIONS OF SHAME AND SELF-BLAME

One far-reaching effect of sexual abuse concerns a sense of guilt or blame: a young child will generally absolve their abuser from blame, internalising that absolution on the basis that it is unsafe, wrong or 'naughty' to blame the parent or the abuser. A child cannot work out how to cope with the awful psychological trauma of abuse. Instead, in order to gain some sense of control, he or she will develop a corresponding sense that the abuse must, in some way, be their fault. This belief is deeply ingrained, almost always unconscious and very firmly held. It is very important to realise this within the therapeutic relationship. Often, adult survivors of childhood abuse wrestle with themselves over blame: part of them will say they realise that the abuse wasn't their fault – but another part will have some misallocated sense that they must have been responsible. We will look at how to help a survivor with this difficulty in Chapter Five.

THE EFFECTS OF CHILDHOOD SEXUAL ABUSE IN ADULTHOOD

Adult survivors of childhood sexual abuse often suffer considerably and in complex ways. About 97%[10] of adults who have suffered abuse are likely to experience some symptoms of post-traumatic stress, where abuse can cause late effects such as:

- recurrent dreams, flashbacks, thoughts and images;
- general stress, anxiety and hypersensitivity to catastrophe or the possibility of catastrophe;
- intense distress at exposure to anything that points to the abuse ('triggers' or 'cues'), even if not consciously remembered;
- difficulty sleeping, concentrating, remembering and using words;
- emotional and social avoidance; difficulty relating, loving and engaging in normal social activities;
- self-harm, alcoholism and substance abuse; increased risk-taking;
- mental illness: depression, feeling suicidal, personality disorders.

It might be helpful for us to consider some of these effects more closely.

FLASHBACKS AND INTRUSIVE MEMORIES

Flashbacks involve a different state of consciousness. Those who suffer them are not just 'imagining' but *re-experiencing* a traumatic event as if it were happening *now*. This can happen when a person is fully conscious or through a nightmare, often as the result of a 'trigger' factor or 'cue'. Flashbacks can be so very real that the sufferer relives all the physical and emotional sensations associated with the trauma: fear, smells, sweating, pain and sounds can reoccur.

Earlier in this chapter, we used the metaphor of a filing cabinet storing information in the brain. Again, a helpful way of understanding the experience of flashbacks is to think of memories as being encoded in the brain, as if in two filing cabinets. One holds normal, processed memories which can be accessed relatively easily, and a second holds traumatic memories. The contents of the second cabinet are not easily accessible because the person has generally done all they can to avoid recalling such memories. But a traumatic memory *can* be triggered by a sensory cue, by an event or during counselling. Suddenly, the drawer to that tightly closed second cabinet is hauled open and those previously inaccessible, painful memories are tipped out unexpectedly and experienced as a flashback.

Flashbacks can be extremely frightening and distressing, so a counsellor will do everything possible to avoid a client reaching the stage where they experience a flashback during a session. However, it *is* necessary to find a way to process those traumatic memories: to help the client to be able to describe (and process) the emotions and feelings associated with the abuse in a healthy way – in other words, to help them move the memories from the second filing cabinet into the first. (In Chapter Five we will consider in more detail how to help a client process memories.)

STRESS

Adult survivors can also exhibit the 'hypervigilance' we mentioned earlier. Finding it hard to trust or believe that the same trauma may not reoccur, they will remain anxious and jumpy, exhibiting the emotional and physical symptoms of stress: muscle aches and pains, diarrhoea, irregular heartbeats, headaches, feelings of panic and fear.

SOCIAL AND EMOTIONAL AVOIDANCE AND DISSOCIATION

Survivors may exhibit emotional and social avoidance: other people are too difficult or too potentially dangerous to cope with. Feelings may be numbed as it is too upsetting for them to experience memories, so in order to cope an effort will be made to feel nothing at all. Survivors may also experience *dissociation*. We all may experience a mild form of dissociation, for example day dreaming, but in the face of trauma a person may experience a partial or complete disruption of their normal, conscious, integrated psychological functioning. Dissociative episodes can be experienced as a 'one-off', as a defence mechanism in response to trauma; or they may present as a more persistent dissociative disorder such as Depersonalisation or Dissociative Identity Disorder (DID).

(Dissociation will be considered in more detail in Chapter Five.)

SELF-HARM

It is possible that a client might disclose that they self-harm – cutting or burning themselves, or pulling out their hair. Research shows that sexual abuse in childhood is often associated with deliberate episodes of self-harm in adult life.[11]

Self-harm is often a response to emotional overload or shut down. It provides release when internal pain becomes unbearable: the physical pain is a temporary distraction and release. So it is important to remember that self-harm is the symptom – not the problem. It is not an act of destruction, but an act of survival.

> Sophie, aged fifteen, began to meet with her school counsellor at the sensitive suggestion of her teacher, who noticed significant scratches on Sophie's arms after asking her to remove a heavy cardigan which was not part of school uniform. Sophie had been self-harming for some weeks and this had coincided with a sharp drop in both her school performance and her behaviour. Sophie eventually disclosed that her father had begun to visit her bedroom at night, and that what had seemingly begun as mild teasing and physical play had developed into more serious sexual abuse. Her disclosure was responded to in accordance with the school's clearly defined confidentiality policy, and she was given support and counselling to help her with the impact of the abuse and her coping strategy of self-harming.

ALCOHOL AND SUBSTANCE MISUSE

Studies have indicated that children who are sexually abused are more likely to have later problems with alcohol and substance abuse. Whilst further research into this area is needed, it appears that alcohol and/or drugs may be used as a coping mechanism in adult life.[12]

FACTORS REGARDING THE IMPACT OF ABUSE

The degree of negative impact of abuse is related to a number of factors:

- The severity of the abuse (although it may be relative, there is, to the client, no 'hierarchy' of abuse);
- The duration – how long it continued: a single incident or frequently;
- The nature of the relationship between the abuser and the client – the closer it is, the more damaging (a parent, for example);
- The age of the victim at the last experience of the abuse – the older a child was, the more difficult and damaging it is to the child's sense of self and their ability to trust others;
- Abuse involving penetration has been closely linked to marital disruption, sexual difficulties and a tendency not to practise religion.

MEDIATING FACTORS

- Causal attribution – if the client is able to rightly locate the blame onto the abuser they are more likely to develop a better self-image beyond the abuse.
- Finding meaning – if the client can find some form of meaning in what happened, it can mediate the damage of the abuse. For example, if a survivor uses their difficult experience in order

to help others.
- Supportive relationships – if the client was supported by one of the parents (especially if they broke the secret of the abuse in childhood), it can mediate the damage.
- Being able to disclose abuse to another person can assist a survivor's resilience to the impact of sexual abuse.

Contemplating the symptoms, effects and impact of sexual abuse on young lives can be harrowing and draining. We would suggest that you take a break from reading at the end of this chapter, remembering that there *is* hope.

In the next chapter, we will move on to look at the therapeutic relationship between client and counsellor or helper, as well as the practical help and support that can be given on the journey beyond sexual abuse.

REFLECTION

Read Psalm 139.

In the context of abuse, this psalm may stir mixed responses within us. On the one hand, we are told that God knows us intimately; that He 'knit [us] together' (v.13). Yet on the other hand it also appears to imply that God knows each moment of our lives with equal intimacy. How does that square up with the experience and impact of abuse? Where was God?

But look more closely at verses 11–12. Might this begin to suggest that when we try to hide in the dark, through fear of being found, through fear of pain, God is with us in that darkest place; that, however terrible that darkness, ultimately He has authority over it?

There are no easy answers – and we should never try to

give them. But perhaps, as we listen to voiced pain, within our desire for understanding we might see a small glimmer of the light of God. And, in so doing, ask Him to bring it into our caring and counselling relationship – even as we examine the harrowing impact and effects of abuse.

PRAYER

Lord of Light,
As what was done in darkness is revealed in the light, may it be Your Light.
Bring wisdom, compassion, empathy and right understanding into the terrible detail I must face with the one I care for.
Not that it be swept away, trivialised or accounted for,
but that it be held in the powerful light of Your love; the One whose humanity knew pain and abuse, and who suffered for us.
Stand with us silently in the lightening shadows, Lord.
Amen.

CHAPTER 4

BEGINNING THE PATH TO HEALING: THE THERAPEUTIC RELATIONSHIP

In this chapter we will begin to explore how we can help a survivor of abuse to find the beginning of a path to healing, the restoration of their sense of self and an ability to rebuild their trust in others. The quality and nature of the helping relationship between the survivor of abuse and the counsellor/helper is a key part of this process.

As we are discussing a therapeutic relationship in this chapter, we will, as suggested earlier, refer to the one who has been abused mainly as the 'client' and the helper as the 'counsellor'. This does not in any way exclude those who do not identify their role in this way, but does emphasise the need for a specialist therapeutic relationship in many situations.

WHO CAN HELP - AND HOW?

This defined mode of reference frames the first question we might ask ourselves: 'Does a survivor need a counsellor who is an expert in the field of sexual abuse?' At the beginning of this book we highlighted the importance of clear roles and boundaries in the accompaniment of the survivors of sexual abuse. Different 'needs' require different responses.

Heather's counselling experience has taught her that the suggestion that a client needs an 'expert' may send a potentially unhelpful message: that the issues stemming from *their* abuse are so alarming and complex that *they* need a specialist. Whilst the issues surrounding abuse are undoubtedly complex, this message can be counterproductive: it reinforces the sense of isolation or of being 'different' that a client who has suffered sexual abuse is already experiencing. It would be easy for them to feel that *we* are out of our depth because they are 'too hot to handle'; a feeling which only adds to their shame and sense of alienation.

Without doubt, counsellors working in this area *do* need to develop an understanding of the effects of abuse and an awareness of the issues involved: sharing of experience, mentoring and education are vital. But the 'who' is not always as simple as it may seem. Assigning an 'expert' may not always be straightforward, as clients frequently don't disclose their history of abuse until, perhaps, the fifth or subsequent session, once a degree of trust and a sense of safety have been established. As we suggested earlier, re-referring at this stage (or suggesting that we can't help so we will find someone who can) could be harmful. It would require the client to start all over again, not only in establishing trust but also in the painful process of retelling their story.

They may feel that repeating the experience is just too much to face and end their search for help.

If we hear an account of abuse as a friend, clergy member or layperson a different dilemma might be faced. We may hear some of the most difficult words we have ever heard, but we must remain open, calm yet concerned; telling the person simply that we find what we've heard distressing, yet without being overly emotional ourselves or expressing shock. The person to whom we are listening needs our compassion, our empathy and our calmness; and to know that what has happened to them was not acceptable under any circumstances. This will validate their experience while also recognising and acknowledging their pain and hurt. It is not for us to pass comment, make judgments, give reasons or add commentary – just to listen, listen and go on listening to the story, however it is told. In a sense, it is our role to 'catch it and hold it', for as long as we are asked to.

Aware that what they'll be disclosing is distressing, survivors of abuse can feel very protective towards their listener. For this reason, they will, quite rightly, often choose to disclose only to someone they believe has the experience to cope: a trained counsellor or someone they know or believe may have experience in this field. By choosing the skill of a professional often *alongside* the care of a friend they are not rejecting the friend's care but, very possibly, protecting him or her.

If, in the early stages of conversation as a friend, clergy member or layperson, we become aware that we are 'out of our depth', we must respond accordingly: recognising that our role as a facilitator is to move someone towards professional counselling, rather than trying to 'do it ourselves'. We may need to gently suggest referral to the person who is disclosing, whilst clearly expressing that we are not giving up or refusing to get involved. It is important to explain that for the best care and outcome to be available, it may be helpful if, together, we find someone who is more experienced and understanding of the issues they face. They may actually (wordlessly or otherwise) be asking us to do just that. We can still help by supporting the counselling process in other ways: by driving them to the counselling appointment or meeting for coffee, all the while reinforcing clear boundaries to each supporting role. Even then, we may need some skilled support or supervision.

Nonetheless, we should *never* underestimate the healing that follows a survivor first feeling heard and believed. We are effectively helping them to break a silence – often about a secret they have kept all their lives. Acceptance, gentleness and compassion can be extremely healing. Likewise, the quality of the trusting relationship between counsellor and client is absolutely vital to the therapeutic success, holding the key to helping a survivor rebuild their ability to trust others. Perhaps that is never more so than in this context: when survivors of abuse have experienced a huge *betrayal* of trust and abuse of relationship.

Mark's form teacher, Jeff, began to feel out of his depth when Mark disclosed an incident of sexual abuse that had occurred at a sports club. Yet Mark had developed a healthy and respectful relationship with Jeff, in whom he trusted. With Mark's permission Jeff mentioned the outline of the situation to his Head of Year, to protect himself and his professional accountability. Having taken expert advice, all involved agreed that the relationship of trust was more important than Jeff's lack of specialist knowledge. Jeff was able to help Mark, with the early supportive involvement of the school counsellor and the police, in order to offer Mark the long-term 'umbrella' support, friendship and security he needed.

FIRST THINGS FIRST: BEFORE WE LISTEN

Trust, as we've mentioned, is paramount in the therapeutic relationship. There are therefore some preliminaries which will help us to both foster trust and set boundaries which offer security to the one we are trying to help.

Firstly, as highlighted earlier, it is important to be clear about what the client is looking for as they share their story. Often it is simply to be heard. At other times they may want us to help them bring a perpetrator of abuse to light or to justice. In this situation, we must reiterate that it is strongly recommended that the police are involved to take a statement *before* any form of helping or counselling begins. This avoids elements of suggestibility which may jeopardise a case. This is both for our own protection and for the protection of the client.

Survivors are often quite anxious about whether a counsellor or helper will be able to offer complete confidentiality as their story is heard. As mentioned in Chapter One, it is helpful for counsellors and helpers to reassure survivors of the following: unless the client divulges that a specific child is at risk of abuse, the counsellor is able to respect disclosure and can be trusted not to break confidentiality, unless they are required to do so by law, for supervision purposes or because of concerns for the client's safety.

As the survivor begins to tell their story, it is sometimes helpful to explain to them how sexual abuse can be related to other problems. Often clients don't recognise any link, so absorbed are they by what has happened to them. But this explanation can help them to disarm what to them seems like an enormous incendiary device – and to defuse it, component by component, making it less dangerous to handle.

Alice came into counselling in her early twenties battling with issues of low self-esteem and poor body image. She had a deep sense of shame about herself as a woman and had been unable to maintain any relationships with the opposite sex, or to join in with the usual 'girlie' and feminine fun (clothes shopping, make-up and 'getting ready for a night out') enjoyed by so many young women of her age. Only after several counselling sessions did she disclose that as a young child she'd been sexually abused by her grandfather on several occasions. Initially she couldn't see the connection. As the weeks went by she was helped to see how the abuse had shattered her own self-image and, eventually, how it might be built up again through confronting what had happened so many years ago and allowing her view of herself as a lovely young woman to be rebuilt.

It is also helpful to explore how willing a client is to look at what happened when they were abused; to affirm that they were *not* in control of their experience as a child but that they *are* in control of what they share of that experience in the counselling process.

This asks the client's permission to talk about what happened and yet, at the same time, provides a safe place for them to share if they choose to do so. What they share comes with a huge expectation of trust. It may take some time for that trust to build to a point, or various points, where they feel able to share the next detail of their story. Time and patience is required – and neither can be measured.

We must prepare the client for what is likely to happen when they talk about the abuse for what is probably the first time; and prepare them (and ourselves) for the inevitable pain involved in the slow healing process. We need to explain that having broken their silence and looked again at what happened to them, they will often feel worse for a time. Reliving traumatic memories can cause strong feelings and powerful emotions to surface – anger, shame, fear – feelings they may have buried for years. In the telling of their story they can feel incredibly physically vulnerable. One of Heather's clients said that she felt stripped naked in doing so, and very vulnerable and shaky afterwards.

Part of the purpose of exploring the abuse is also to allow a necessary process of grief over a lost childhood or formative years. Grief, as we know, is hard, emotional and physical work and cannot be hurried. We need to take time and space to listen as much as possible in these early stages, whilst not allowing the client to become overwhelmed by too much too soon. In listening to the stories of abuse we need wisdom – as much in knowing where to stop for a while as in knowing how to make a start.

HISTORY TAKING: HEARING THE STORY OF ABUSE

Our relationship as listener is likely to be for the long haul. What the client needs is consistency, trust, belief and someone who is prepared to go the distance.

Disclosing the story of abuse can be painful. Shame, guilt, stigma and fear of not being believed, or of the repercussions of revealing what is secret, can make beginning to open up fraught with difficulty. Many survivors will have found it difficult to integrate what has happened to them into the rest of their lives (even into their personalities) because they have been unable to share their experiences. Sharing their story is therefore an important part of helping them to wholeness.

Telling our life story – in whatever situation and whatever it includes – is part of affirming who we are and of placing ourselves in the world. Telling the story of abuse may not be done from start to finish but in fragments of memory, pictures or snatches of activity and dialogue. One memory may trigger another; one question may halt the story or move it on. It is worth re-emphasising then that on this particular journey we tread carefully, even in our listening.

We can sometimes hesitate to ask about the details of abuse for fear of being too suggestive, of causing distress or even of silencing the client. So, we need to avoid intrusive questions while, as we mentioned earlier, giving permission for the client to share as and what they can.

There can be a number of reasons why someone is reluctant to share details of abuse:

- shame – often based on a perceived failure to stop the abuse;
- self-blame;

- fear of rejection;
- wish to avoid the memory;
- fear of being labelled a potential abuser themselves;
- wish to protect the abuser;
- for men – the desire to conform to the internalised social stereotype of needing to be strong, not a victim;
- fear of splitting up the family – it may be easier to play along and suffer in silence.

Children have more complex problems in that they:
- may not know what is wrong, or see the behaviour as 'normal';
- may be unable to explain what has happened;
- may fear retaliation or reoccurrence if they tell;
- may fear the loss of someone they love or the loss of their home and security, where abuse in the family is concerned.

They may have been told that they will not be believed or that the abuse is their fault, and so be reluctant to disclose details of their experience. Almost 80% of children, when abuse comes to light, initially deny abuse or are reluctant to disclose: 75% disclose accidentally.[1]

THE LISTENER'S RESPONSE
We have considered what our general response should be to hearing the story of abuse. What might be more specifically unhelpful or helpful?

UNHELPFUL RESPONSES

These words may make us wince, but all of the following responses have been known by Heather to have been used by 'helpers'. It might be helpful for us to consider how each might impact the client of abuse:

- Disbelief: 'Well you were young – are you sure it happened?'
- 'Why didn't you stop it?'
- 'It was just a game, I expect!'
- Asking intrusive or intense questions too early in the counselling relationship;
- Minimising the importance of the abuse: 'Well it doesn't matter'; 'It happened a long time ago, didn't it? Let's look at the present!'
- Shock/disgust. The 'Oh my God!' response;
- Touching the speaker;
- 'You just need to pray, forgive and move on.'

HELPFUL RESPONSES

- Remaining very calm;
- Visible, and again calm, concern. (By being calm we are sending the message that we can contain this.)
- Gentleness;
- Acknowledging the difficulty of disclosure: 'This must be so hard for you ...'
- Affirming the client for having done this: 'You're being very brave in sharing this and trusting me with it. Thank you.'
- Allowing the client to disclose at their own pace; very gently exploring: 'Take your time, I'm listening.'
- Being wholly supportive;
- Asking them how they feel after the disclosure: 'How do you feel now?'

- Attending to immediate resulting physical needs by asking them what they feel in their body 'at the moment';
- Exploring what support is available between sessions. (Those who have kept a secret for years feel incredibly exposed and vulnerable when they have broken the silence. Looking at the support they may have available before meeting again is important.)

REVIEWING ASPECTS OF THE ABUSE

Listening means remembering, and it will be important for us to gain as clear a picture as possible of the abuse we are hearing about. We will need to help the client to piece together the fragments of their experience in order to process it, integrate what has happened into the rest of their lives and receive some measure of healing from the abusive experience.

So, we need to be clear about:

- The age at which the abuse started;
- The duration – was it once or twice, or did it go on for years?
- The number of abusers. (We shouldn't assume that there was only one: abusers are very good at identifying vulnerable children.)
- The relationship to the abuser. (The closer the relationship the more damaging: an abusive father is devastating.)
- What happened and what was said. It's helpful to very gently try to find out what the abuser *said* because this is often what clients are saying to themselves, perhaps unconsciously: 'This is your fault'; 'You deserve this.'
- Did any of the family members know?
- Were any other family members abused – or anyone else in the community?

- What ended the abuse? Has it ended? (Don't assume if you have an adult client that it *has* ended.)

Having heard the story (and it will unfold, backtrack and develop in more detail in subsequent sessions), we then have the difficult task of addressing the issues raised by the abuse in the life of the client. These can be huge and complex, often overlapping and inter-tangling. Issues can be physical, emotional, sexual, social, spiritual, philosophical and even intellectual – especially where the use of power and control is concerned.

> Emily struggled with very particular 'cues' which reminded her of the sexual abuse she had suffered at the hands of her father in her childhood years. He would generally enter her bedroom when his favourite TV programmes had finished, two or three times a week. This meant that not only were the closing theme tunes of three particular TV programmes a 'cue' that the abuse was likely to happen, but each was a cue for fear and anxiety, even twenty years later. Over several months, Emily's counsellor used DVDs of the programmes to help Emily revisit both the cues and the memories until they no longer held such power over her memory and imagination.

In the next two chapters we will consider the issues related to abuse in terms of the Waverley Model:
- physical
- emotional
- volitional – how they behave

- rational – what they think
- spiritual – their relationship with God and how they find meaning in life.

We'll begin to look at how we can help clients practically in the context of the shared therapeutic relationship, as we accompany them on the next stage of their journey.

REFLECTION

Return to the story of Jesus' meeting with the Samaritan woman in John 4:1–42.

If you look more closely you may notice that this 'listening relationship' carries the following hallmarks:

- Focused listening
- Honesty
- Mutual respect
- Freedom of choice
- An exploration of faith
- The restoration of self-worth, liberty and hope.

Whilst we cannot draw parallels between every aspect of this story and our work with the abused, there are some clear pointers for the therapeutic relationship which 'listens to a life'.

Earlier, we mentioned that 'to be heard is to know dignity restored'. As we listen, we take our eyes – and ears – off ourselves (whilst maintaining a necessary degree of self-awareness) in an atmosphere of great trust, as we help our client to break a long-held silence.

What have you learned from watching Jesus in this account that you can take into your own listening?

PRAYER

God of relationship,
I invite You to be at the centre of every meeting of heart, mind and story.
To hold for us all pain, guilt, anger and shame.
As I listen,
fill my heart with compassion,
my mind with discernment,
and my (almost still) lips with wisdom.
Amen.

CHAPTER 5

ADDRESSING THE IMPACT OF PHYSICAL, BEHAVIOURAL AND EMOTIONAL DIFFICULTIES

Sexual abuse is *never* without consequences.

Research indicates that the impact of childhood sexual abuse extends well into adult life[1], leaving those who have been abused to face a variety of physical, behavioural and emotional issues that inevitably impact every area of their lives. Often they are unaware that an issue with which they are struggling has some connection to the abuse they have suffered. Sometimes they might identify a link but feel powerless to change anything for the better. As accompaniers on their journey we can help survivors of sexual abuse untangle the complexity of the resulting issues they face, so clearing the way ahead.

In this chapter we will look at some of the common physical, behavioural and emotional issues faced by clients, and consider how both these issues and the resulting needs might be helped within the therapeutic or caring relationship.

ADDRESSING PHYSICAL ISSUES

The memory of abuse may often mean that a client finds any kind of physical contact or intervention extremely difficult. This can result in a lack of self-care, since medical examinations or dental examinations (even trips to the hairdresser or beauty salon) can be traumatic. There is a fear of any intrusive procedure or activity which resembles the abuse or in which the client feels out of control of the circumstances or behaviour.

> Louise suffered recurring dental and gum disease problems in her twenties because she hadn't ever visited the dentist as an adult and could only just bring herself to brush her teeth. Her last visit, as a teenager, had been so traumatic that she had failed to return. Louise found any kind of situation in which she was a passive participant difficult anyway, but the very thought of the dentist's approach terrified her. As an eleven-year-old she had been forced to have oral sex with an uncle on several occasions and consequently had been left with an inability to eat some foods or to have anything remain in her mouth for any length of time. Louise was eventually helped by a counsellor who taught her relaxation techniques and by a programme of gradually lengthened visits to a dentist who specialised in nervous patients.

Clients will often experience self-loathing – hating their body, not wanting to care for it or seeing it in some way as having betrayed them. Often they will choose to dress in dark or voluminous clothes in order either to cover it or to draw attention away from it. They might wash excessively or avoid mirrors. Abuse can distort body image to such a degree that the most attractive person can sincerely believe that they are hideously ugly.

To be touched unexpectedly can trigger flashbacks, and cause distress or flinching physical withdrawal, dizziness, even nausea and sickness. Activities as simple as standing in a crowded underground train or being unexpectedly kissed in friendly greeting can prove traumatic. We need to remember this when helping survivors. Counsellors do not usually touch clients, but in the context of prayer ministry helpers will often put their hands on the shoulders or arms of those for whom they are praying. We would recommend that the recipient's consent is always granted before a reassuring touch of hand or arm is given during prayer ministry. Prayer facilitators and counsellors generally do not (and cannot) know who has been abused and who has not, so great care needs to be taken not to touch the person in case a memory is triggered. Such consent may even be framed in the *survivor's* request for a reassuring hug or a hand to hold. Either way, care must always be taken and consent must always remain with the one we are helping.

ADDRESSING EMOTIONAL ISSUES

The nature and trauma of sexual abuse means that most counselling work will be done in the area of the emotions. The journey (through what is nothing less than the emotional wreckage wrought by abuse) can be difficult and traumatic; it is not to be undertaken lightly. It is important to understand some of the pathways, processes and methods needed to live with the aftermath of sexual abuse; and the ways in which we can help move clients to a safer emotional place.

Our first task is to help and encourage the client to express their myriad of emotions – anger, guilt, fear, shame – and to verbalise them. A child will rarely have the skills to cope with the feelings that surround abuse. Instead they will often deny or dissociate it to survive. If they are very young they may not have the capacity even to identify feelings. Revisiting – and to some extent helping them remember what happened very gently – can help them to identify and express feelings about what happened to them. BUT we must take care. This path can lead to great anxiety, so it is essential that it is only taken at the client's pace and with their permission.

Such disclosure often begins with an initial struggle with a sense of shame.

RESPONDING TO SHAME, ANGER AND GUILT

Clients (both adult and child) often replay internalised messages about their experience of abuse; messages which carry a deep sense of shame and guilt, and which say: 'I am to blame; this was my fault.' Abusers will often have told them that they *are* to blame, using phrases such as: 'You made me'; 'You asked for it'; 'You enjoyed it'; all of which reinforce that belief. As we mentioned earlier, there can be a gap between head and heart. While a client's head tells them that they cannot, either circumstantially, morally or logically, be to blame, in their heart they believe that they were, in some way, responsible for what happened. Often they feel this simply because they did not put a stop to the abuse – even if they'd been completely unable to do so. Frequently asked questions are: 'Why didn't I stop it?' 'Why didn't I tell others?' Helping them to understand that, as a child, trying to stop the abuse is simply too frightening can help them to recognise that they did not have the power to do so.

Clients may also need to be reminded that if the abuse was perpetrated by a close member of the family, disclosing would have interfered with their basic need to maintain a loving relationship within that family. This is such an overwhelming need that they would have been powerless to tell anyone for fear of losing the stability and love they knew. Once clients can begin to realise this – and also to understand that often the only way a child can cope with trauma is to blame themselves – it becomes possible for them to begin the journey of transferring the culpability onto the abuser.

A distorted perception of self in childhood means that clients will often have an extremely poor self-image, using words to describe themselves such as: 'worthless', 'bad', 'evil', 'dirty', 'rubbish', 'unlovable'. Some of these 'labels' will have been heard, others assumed.

In an attempt to survive, clients are often seen driving themselves to succeed in adult life, professionally or otherwise, to somehow cover what they believe to be the 'truth': that deep down they are unacceptable and worthless. Clients are thus often involved in a constant search to find out who they are – in an effort to feel, and be, more than just a surviving victim.

We will consider how to help a survivor with this difficulty in Chapter Six. However, at this point, we cannot stress strongly enough how important it is that a counsellor or helper affirms *again and again that the abuse was not the client's fault.* This cannot be done as a 'one off' or a quick fix. It can take a long time to relocate the blame rightly onto the abuser. We need to remember that we are in the process of rebuilding, brick by fragile brick, a wall of innocence and worth that has been bulldozed by abuse.

When clients begin to talk about the abuse they suffered, they often find that anger surfaces, sometimes for the first time. Helping a client to express their anger will be an important part of the recovery process. Yvonne Dolan gives her book *Beyond Survival* the subtitle, *Living Well is the Best Revenge* and suggests that being able to 'live well' beyond abuse is the best form of response to anger and the need for revenge.[2]

Clients may also get very muddled over guilt and false guilt, often expressing guilt related to events that they were powerless to control. It is often necessary to help a client explore what might be *legitimate* guilt (eg throwing a brick at a car because they were so angry) and *false* guilt (ie the sexual abuse).

PRACTICAL AND CREATIVE THERAPEUTIC APPROACHES

ADDRESSING THE CHILD

In adulthood it helps to encourage the client to gain an adult perspective on what happened to them in the abusive situation. Often, because of the internal messages and labels we mentioned earlier, clients will have an inaccurate perception of what they could or could not have done about the abuse, as children. It can therefore be helpful to ask the client to think of a child of a similar age now to the age they were at the time of the abuse. This often helps the survivor to be able to more easily identify with their own 'inner' child. Then we might ask: 'What would happen if that child came into the room now, crying and saying to us both that she has been abused?' 'How do you feel about her and what she is telling you?' 'What would you like to say to her now?'

This is a powerful exercise. It can often help the client to say both what she would like to have been said to her as a child and can also help the client to gain an adult perspective on what happened in childhood.

(NOTE: *This exercise needs to be chosen and used sensitively* and may not always be appropriate. In introducing this exercise, we are clearly *not* asking the client to think of a child they know who *may be, has been* or is *actually being* abused, rather for them to think of a child they know who is a similar *age* to them when *they* were abused, in order to help them identify with a child who is at the same age as when they were first abused.)

It may also be helpful for the client to use photographs of themselves at the age at which the abuse took place. As they look at their own image they can be encouraged to say what they would want to say to themselves in that situation. This can be hugely emotive, as it can raise unexpected, as well as long and deeply held, questions: questions that even the client did not realise they wanted to ask and which enable the child in the photograph to say what they hadn't been able to say at the time. It allows both child and adult to be heard: an essential part of the process of disclosing and moving on with the memory of abuse.

Amanda was encouraged to bring photographs of herself as a child to her counselling sessions. One particular photograph she found very difficult to look at as it showed her wearing a particular dress which reminded her vividly of aspects of the abuse. However, she persevered. As the exploring of painful events proceeded, Amanda took the voice of herself as a child and was able to protest, answer back and, eventually, place the blame rightly on her abuser. For Amanda the session was an emotional, but positively releasing, turning point.

BIBLIOTHERAPY

In sharing their own story, clients might also find it helpful to read stories of other adults who have survived abuse. Care should be taken that this is encouraged at the right time. If stories are used at an appropriate stage they can be helpful in ending a sense of isolation and be the beginning of helping a client to see the possibility of healing and recovery after suffering the experience of abuse. Stories can also be helpful in identifying feelings through empathy and in the process of redistributing blame.

USING ART

One creative intervention is to ask the client to draw themselves and the abuser. This can often reveal details or strong elements of focus that they find difficult to verbalise or understand. Drawing the abuser as much larger than themselves may express the sense of power the abuser had over them. Including small details, objects or environment may highlight cues or triggers which aid memory and understanding.

COPING WITH ANXIETY/TRAUMA

In Chapter Three, we mentioned flashbacks and noted that for some clients processing the memories of abuse is traumatic. Therefore, as the abuse is explored, it can mean working in the realm of trauma management, requiring the expertise of an experienced therapist. Consequently, we are *not* suggesting in the following pages that helpers or novice counsellors should engage in this work. Instead, they would be wise to seek help from an experienced therapist. However, if a survivor begins to share their story and, whilst doing so, demonstrates signs of increased anxiety or hyperventilation, or experiences the memory as though it were currently happening, there are some simple grounding techniques we can use to help the survivor in those moments.

If a counsellor or helper senses (or the client suggests) that a memory is becoming overwhelming, grounding techniques can be used to restore calm:

1. In reminding the client that they are in a safe place, the counsellor might suggest that the client describes something physical (for example, the chair they are sitting in), while asking closed questions: 'Is the chair hard or soft?' 'What colour is it?'

2. The counsellor might ask the client to open their eyes and maintain eye contact.

3. While remaining very calm themselves a counsellor might help a client to slow down their breathing. Talking to them slowly and calmly, the counsellor may suggest that they

breathe slowly in and out, perhaps placing their hands on their stomach to feel each breath. (Avoid any unhelpful physical 'cues' or triggers.)

4. The counsellor may ask further closed questions: 'Are you feeling cold?' 'Is that sunlight too bright for you?' 'Can you hear the traffic outside?' These questions can help to bring the anxious person back to the present time and place.

5. It is also helpful to teach a client some of the above grounding techniques to help them cope if they have to deal with a flashback outside the session.

6. Another method is to teach the imagining of a safe and reassuring place to which the client can mentally 'go' in order to stop the flashback. Or to imagine that feelings and memories are being locked in a box and contained – just for a short while – until those memories can be released and dealt with in a safer place.

7. The counsellor might need to decide, together with the client, that, if the memories are just too difficult to cope with alone, for now, they will only be looked at together in an accepted 'safe place' (eg inside the counselling room).

NOTE: We must reiterate that these techniques and strategies should generally only be used by a skilled counsellor (or in emergency situations *only* by an untrained counsellor or helper) and always approached *with great caution*.

PROCESSING AND REINTEGRATING MEMORIES

As explained earlier, memories will often need to be revisited, processed and reintegrated in order to facilitate progress. So the counsellor's goal is not to *suppress* memories, but to help a client to experience and process them, while explaining to the client that in doing so, however frightening the experience, the intense pain of the memory will not last forever. It is really important to realise that the process of reintegrating memories takes time. As ever, there is no quick fix, but healing *can* be found.

DISSOCIATIVE DISORDERS

We know that sometimes children are so unable to cope with what is happening to them that they 'dissociate' themselves from it.

Dissociation (rather than *disassociation*) is an adaptive response to extreme trauma. Essentially, a child switches off to escape the inescapable. They may even describe how they 'leave their body behind'. As a survival strategy, this can be very helpful in childhood but in adult life it can seriously impair healthy functioning, causing fragmentation of the personality.

Mental health is seen as a continuum. As we know, some dissociation is 'normal': we can get 'lost' in a book or a film, in music or reverie. So, at one end of the continuum, someone with a healthy normal personality (in touch with the world and with other people around him/her) can at times dissociate. However, at the other extreme is the person with dissociative or dissociation identity disorder (DID). DID (previously known as Multiple Personality Disorder) is a mental health difficulty which presents as a reaction to severe trauma in early childhood, often the trauma of extreme sexual or emotional abuse. Dissociating at the extreme end of the continuum results in a serious inability to function: a person can have separate entities, or mental states, which take on identities and personalities of their own. A psychiatric diagnosis of DID is made when the parts or personalities completely take control of a person's behaviour.

Somewhere between these two ends of the continuum lie survivors who, in childhood, dissociated to cope with the trauma of abuse. For example, during a traumatic experience of abuse, a person may 'disconnect' as they mentally escape from the pain and fear of the trauma. Because this process produces changes in memory, people who dissociate can often find that their sense of who they are and of what happened to them is profoundly affected. When in process, dissociation disables any connections between thoughts, memories and feelings. Episodes can be brief and relatively normal (like daydreams) or extreme and lengthy (usually where there are mental health issues).

When a child is faced with an overwhelming traumatic situation, this disconnection facilitates a defence against acute physical and/or emotional pain, enabling the child to function as if the trauma had not occurred and, therefore, to survive. If a child is repeatedly abused, however, the dissociation becomes reinforced and conditioned.

Not all survivors of sexual abuse will have difficulties with dissociation and many of us, as counsellors or helpers, will not need to manage this disorder in a therapeutic or caring situation. But it is important to be aware of the possibility. It is possible that we will be told by a client that they have coped by 'disconnecting', 'distancing themselves' or 'going away'. Often they will describe themselves 'floating' apart from their body. At an unconscious level they will have been saying to themselves that they will not remember; that they cannot survive the feelings so they will not make them theirs.

Such survival strategies can be seen as falling into two categories:

1. Denial – 'It didn't really happen' or
2. Dissociation – 'It happened to someone else'

FACILITATING REINTEGRATION: PRACTICAL POINTERS

Dissociation can present as the client having 'blank spells', becoming dazed or trance-like when emotions are heightened. If this happens as a counsellor listens to the client (and in assessing this he/she may identify more nonverbal clues than verbal), it can be helpful to stop the session, bring the client back to the present moment and ask them what was happening just a few moments earlier. It can also be helpful to explore memory of the dissociation as it occurred during the abuse experiences, in order to establish which childhood 'coping strategies' were used.

The ultimate aim is to allow emerging memories to be processed without the client dissociating.

NIGHTMARES AND PERCEPTUAL DISTURBANCES

Clients can often be troubled by nightmares about or related to the abuse. It can therefore be helpful to explore dreams – perhaps drawing them with pencil and paper – while giving reassurance that bad dreams are a normal and healthy part of the brain trying to process the memories.

Perceptual disturbances (seeing, hearing, imagining and even smelling and tasting things related to the experience of abuse) are also common. The client might start to imagine that someone is watching them, feel that someone is close to them, smell an aftershave or hear a voice. Again this is a normal part of reliving trauma and will end when memories are processed and reintegrated.

SELF-HARM

In effect, self-harm is a combination of the physical, emotional and behavioural response to sexual abuse by a victim or client, and is very common amongst teenagers. It is important to point out that not every person who self-harms has suffered sexual abuse. Neither does every person who has been sexually abused engage in self-harm. Nevertheless, sexual abuse in childhood is frequently associated with later deliberate episodes of self-harm in adult life and therefore we have included mention of the difficulty in this chapter.

In self-harming an unspoken statement about emotional turmoil is often being made. For example, self-harming which makes the following statements is a result of a 'shutdown' response:

'I self-harm to stay alive – to prove to myself that I am not dead.'

'Cutting saved my life: it makes my life somehow feel more real.'

'I'm numb, so I sit here with a razor: it's something I must do.'

Alternatively, the following statements demonstrate an experience of an 'emotional overload' response:

'I cut myself to get rid of the evil and dirt in me: it's the only way I can get it out.'

'I cannot control the pain: cutting helps me feel as though I am in control.'

'I am rubbish: I deserve to be punished.'

Our goal when faced with incidences of self-harm is to help the self-harmer to express their feelings in a healthy way. Firstly, it is important to understand that self-harm is seen as a form of survival, giving much-needed release or control. It should therefore be understood as a *symptom*, not the problem. Self-harm is not usually an act of destruction but a way of surviving. This can be very hard to understand, but it means that our goal is not necessarily to help the client to *stop* harming, but to help them to *gradually* find an alternative way to express the feelings that have led to the self-harm. Forcing a person to stop self-harming may result in someone swapping one self-harming action for another that is far more damaging.

PRACTICAL RESPONSES TO SELF-HARM

In helping self-harmers to understand what had led to the practice, counsellors and helpers need to develop an understanding of the need for such a painful response. Working together in discovering this can be hugely supportive for the client. Listening well will mean working to identify triggers for self-harm in order to divert the trigger-response towards more appropriate expressive behaviour.

Progress towards rechannelling self-harm more appropriately will involve enabling the articulation of the cause of emotional shutdown or overload. Once again we are asked to listen, listen ... and listen some more.

UNHELPFUL RESPONSES TO SELF-HARM

- A shocked, angry or disapproving reaction

- Criticism – regarding self-harm as attention seeking
- 'Contracts' that insist a person agrees not to self-harm
- Minimising or dismissing self-injuries

HELPFUL RESPONSES TO SELF-HARM
- Being warm, accepting and supportive of the client
- Taking self-harm seriously – facing it *with* the client
- Responding with empathy and conveying concern
- Thinking of self-harm as a consequence of the sexual abuse trauma
- Exploring 'triggers' to self-harm
- Exploring existing coping strategies and establishing new and supportive ones
- Helping the client to admit to self-harm, bringing the 'secret' world of self-harm into the counselling room

FOR THE COUNSELLOR
- To manage the feelings that cutting or other forms of self-injury evoke by taking them to professional supervision and discussing them in depth

We have touched on just a few of the physical, emotional and behavioural issues faced by those who have been abused and have shared some pointers which counsellors might use in responding well. These issues are, by nature, complex and are certainly not exhaustive. Many will overlap and have a close relationship with the issues we will examine in the next chapter: issues that are rational, relational, sexual and spiritual.

REFLECTION

It is when we are physically faced with the suffering of another that we are so often moved to compassion. Frederick Buechner, in *Beyond Words,*[3] writes:

> Compassion is sometimes the fatal capacity for feeling what it is like to live inside somebody else's skin. It is the knowledge that there can never be any peace and joy for me until there is peace and joy finally for you too.

Read 2 Corinthians 1:3–7.

How do Buechner's words correlate with what Paul says about the nature of compassion?

How might each both help and hinder us, as we seek to help others living with the physical, emotional and behavioural effects of sexual abuse?

PRAYER

God of both suffering and compassion,
as I stand alongside those who suffer from the effects of abuse,
transform my compassion with Your love and insight.
May I pour gentleness on the scars of harsh realities;
wait patiently in the slow unfolding of a story;
offer gracious acceptance to the reticence of self-rejection;
and bring true hope into a place of despair.
Amen.

CHAPTER 6

ADDRESSING RATIONAL (COGNITIVE), RELATIONAL, SEXUAL AND SPIRITUAL ISSUES

Experience of abuse inevitably impacts the way clients both think about themselves and relate to others. This chapter examines issues of a client's self-image and belief systems; their relationships with others, including the impact of abuse on sexual relationships; their relationship with their abuser; and the impact of abuse on a survivor's spirituality and faith.

ABUSE AND SELF-BELIEF
The low self-esteem and negative body image which stem from abuse frequently lead to a survivor's genuine belief that they are 'unlovable', 'horrible' or 'disgusting' etc. Compounded by issues of guilt and shame, and by negative self-messages (the internal working model), this means that beliefs are absorbed and taken

(often at a subconscious level) into adult life.

Survivors of abuse often believe that they are 'evil' – a misconception drawn from an assumption that they were chosen by the abuser not because they were vulnerable, but because they were, in some way, flawed or marked out. If there has been more than one abuser such a belief becomes reinforced. For this reason, it is helpful to assist the client in understanding that an offender sees a child as vulnerable; and that abusing them is a misuse of power and control, not an indication that the child is in any way 'flawed' or 'evil'.

Much of the work to be done between client and counsellor, or carer, in this area will be around issues of self-worth and core beliefs about self. Helping survivors to confront and challenge the negative core beliefs they hold about themselves can be easier said than done. In part, this is often because core beliefs are generally entrenched and, even when unhelpful and negative, can be central to a person's sense of self. In addition, these beliefs are often rigid, inflexible and considered by the person to be absolutely true.

So, how can counsellors, and carers, help?

1. Firstly, it will be very helpful for a client to understand that negative core beliefs are usually formed in childhood, often as a result of difficult early life relationships or the traumatic events (such as sexual abuse) they have experienced.

2. Secondly, gently suggesting to a client that they take a 'stand back' viewpoint (perhaps by encouraging them to objectively give examples of when the core belief might not be true) may also start the process of being able to challenge that belief.

For example, if the core belief is 'I am unlovable', we could ask the client when this has *not* been true. In other words, we might ask them when they or others have demonstrated that they *are* lovable. This will start to shake the foundations of negative belief.

3. Thirdly, this is rarely a 'Damascus Road' experience: it usually takes time and great patience. But as the counsellor models acceptance and love towards the client *alongside* this process, the client will hopefully begin the journey towards believing that they are a lovable person, after all. In providing space to examine and dispute false beliefs about self and worth, the survivor is helped to take another step towards healing and the restoration of a healthy self-image.

RELATIONSHIPS WITH OTHERS

Survivors of abuse often demonstrate a reluctance to let other people draw close, both through an inability to trust and in the genuine belief that any relationship would be short-lived once 'they know what I am really like'. On the one hand, there is a deep need to be loved and affirmed and, on the other, an intense fear of rejection. Trust is such a difficult issue that the client will often believe that remaining alone is the only source of safety and security. They would rather withdraw or stay withdrawn than risk being hurt, inevitably increasing the sense of isolation resulting from the abuse. However, research[1] suggests that helping someone to become more connected to others has significant benefits, enabling the person to gain a greater sense of purpose and meaning, as well as assisting them to emotionally connect with others and take better care of themselves. In addition, having social relationships in adult life has been shown to moderate the damage done by external stressful events, such as sexual abuse in childhood.[2]

This presents a further key task for those who help: to assist the survivor to find ways of forming new relationships with others and establishing a social support network. In addition, if the client has been helped to develop a realistic, healthy and positive sense of self they will recognise that they *do* have something to offer in relationships and can begin to learn to trust themselves, and others, in the context of those relationships.

(Self-esteem is explored in more detail in the companion volume, *Insight into Self-Esteem*[3].)

ADDRESSING ISSUES OF SEX AND SEXUALITY

Those who have experienced abuse will often have difficulty in expressing their sexuality or in dealing with sexual feelings, however close their emotional relationship to another person becomes. This can be as much of an issue for a loving partner who cannot understand what they perceive as rejection, as for the survivors themselves. Skilled counselling can be very effective in helping couples to move forward together into understanding, trust (which is paramount) and a fulfilling sexual relationship.

WAYS TO HELP WITH SEXUAL DIFFICULTIES

It is up to client and counsellor to decide whether the issues presented, especially those impacting relationships, might benefit from specialist couple counselling or help from a therapist who is an expert in overcoming sexual difficulties. However, listed opposite are some simple things which might be helpful for clients when they are facing problems – related to earlier abuse –

which surface in their own healthy sexual relationships.

- Firstly, suggesting that clients simply open their eyes if memories or feelings become difficult when they are engaging in sex with their partner can be of value. It can also be very helpful for them to remind themselves that they are with someone they trust and love and who trusts and loves them; that they are making love, not being re-abused.

- Secondly, asking a partner to avoid any triggers which remind the client of abuse – perhaps drinking alcohol or using aftershave, or avoiding a particular place or routine – might also help. It is important to build a store of new, personal, positive and specific memories in what is a loving sexual relationship: this can help to fade memories of abuse.

- Helping a partner be aware of control issues is also vital. Helping the client remember that they *weren't* in control when they were being abused in childhood, and helping them to, in some way, experience control in the loving sexual experience now; both are very important. This may involve time and patience, but being able to be free to ask their partner to stop for a moment, or to do, or not do, a particular thing, while being heard and understood more broadly and deeply, can be incredibly helpful to the sexual relationship. In addition, helping the partner to realise how vital the power issue is will be essential to any progress being made. Otherwise, the dynamics of the abuse can easily be re-experienced and felt by the survivor as though the abuse is being re-enacted.

INVOLUNTARY AROUSAL

Often clients will disclose a feeling of shame and guilt because they remember responding sexually to the abuse they suffered. For example, a boy might have had an erection or a girl describe memories of sexual arousal as a child. As we mentioned earlier, it is important to reassure clients that this is natural, to the extent that we are designed to find sex pleasurable and that these feelings and genital sensitivities to touch begin in childhood. This means that it is the *context* of the response or feeling, not the *feeling* itself, that is wrong. It is the abuser, not the abused, who is wholly responsible for that context; and it is the abuser who wrongly exploits what is a precious gift outside its intended place.

Gary came to counselling in some confusion, having experienced some sexual arousal whilst being sexually abused. He disclosed during therapy that he had experienced an erection during late childhood abuse and wrongly believed that it must have been as a result of personal enjoyment. Yet he hated it. The counsellor explained that what he had experienced was a normal physiological response to being touched in the genital area. It was not an indication that he had enjoyed or sought the experience. Knowing that his response was physiological rather than psychological or sexual greatly helped him to resolve the issue that had been troubling him.

THE SURVIVOR'S RELATIONSHIP TO THEIR ABUSER

It would be easy to believe that a survivor would want nothing more to do with the perpetrator of the abuse they have suffered – and this might be the case. But, despite the nature of what has happened, it has happened in the context of a relationship, however flawed, unwanted or fraught with fear and bewilderment. Often then, clients who are survivors of abuse will consider that there is unfinished business between themselves and their abuser. They have questions, important to their recovery, that they want answered by the abuser. They may also seek some kind of retribution or justice. For a few, this may result in the abuser facing a police enquiry and/or imprisonment; for others, resolution may come partly through expressing their feelings about what took place to the abuser, either directly or indirectly.

However, we must be alert to the fact that if the client wishes to confront their abuser, such confrontation has the potential to be extremely challenging. Often there can be unforeseen consequences. In other words, whilst it might seem like a good idea for the survivor to face their abuser and ask questions or express their feelings of anger, hurt, pain etc, it can easily 'backfire' on the client, compounding suffering and reversing progress. For example, it is quite possible that the abuser might maintain that the abuse didn't happen; or that they were not to blame; or that the survivor was to blame. In these cases, confrontation can be devastating for the survivor. Far from helping them to be able to move on, such an encounter can compound a sense of isolation and the feeling of not being heard or believed. Therefore, it can be helpful for the counsellor

97

to talk through with the survivor what they might want to say. Alternatively, the counsellor might ask the survivor to include it in the form of a letter to the abuser, on the agreement that it will *not* be sent without first exploring, thoroughly, what might happen if it were sent. This should include the consideration of various outcomes: for example, the abuser's denial that the abuse occurred. (This exercise is also particularly helpful if the abuser is no longer alive or their whereabouts unknown.)

It is important to remember that any decisions about confrontation should rest with the client. They should never feel that they have been persuaded or influenced by their counsellor or, for that matter, by their friends and/or relatives. Abuse is about power – and we need to give that power back to the one who has been abused. First and foremost, any confrontation should be about the needs of the abused, not the abuser. Its aim is not necessarily forgiveness, but the redistribution of power; being heard, and re-establishing a sense of security and worth. (We will address the issue of forgiveness in the next chapter.)

Cora had been abused in childhood by her uncle. During the first session she stated that the trigger for beginning counselling was the death of her uncle. Cora tearfully explained that, now he was dead, not only could she not ask the question 'Why?' but her uncle's death had 'closed the door' to her being able to tell him how angry she was at the hurt and pain his abuse had caused. As counselling progressed, the counsellor suggested that Cora tried writing a letter to her uncle, setting out all she'd wanted to say to him, were he still alive. Cora brought this to the next session. She described to her counsellor how helpful the exercise had been in helping her to express some of her feelings about the damage the abuse had done in her life. As the sessions progressed, the counsellor asked Cora what she would like to do with the letter. Together they explored how Cora wanted to burn the letter as a symbol of freeing herself from the power of the abuse. Cora did so, and came to the next session saying that she'd felt a sense of 'freedom' that she had not felt before.

ADDRESSING SPIRITUAL ISSUES: WHERE IS GOD IN ABUSE?

The use of spiritual and faith interventions in counselling is fraught with ethical and personal difficulties of which all involved must be aware.

Firstly, we would recommend that there should be a clear discussion between the client and counsellor with an open agreement/contract about the use of any appropriate sharing of faith and use of spiritual interventions, such as prayer or use of Bible passages. It is also important to recognise that in professional counselling, at least, there is an ethical obligation to work with and fully respect a client's own belief system. In order to work collaboratively, a counsellor would be wise to wait to introduce a spiritual perspective into the counselling conversation until the *client* starts to raise the issue themselves. Once this happens, a clear understanding of relevance and a framework for use can be established.

Survivors who *do* hold religious and spiritual beliefs can struggle with intensely powerful and difficult issues in these areas which are frequently brought into the counselling room.

In addition, as the sexual abuse begins to be explored, clients who are Christians often experience a crisis of faith. As issues are raised and anger expressed, the feelings and questions are often directed at God as well as at the abuser; sometimes perhaps even more at God: 'Why didn't God stop the abuse?' 'Why did God seem distant?' 'Where is the justice in all of this?' 'Why did God let me suffer?' When asking this kind of question, clients generally reveal that they long to know God and to engage Him in dialogue about the abuse; and yet, paradoxically, they have frequent feelings of being abandoned or ignored by Him.[4]

Clients need to be able to ask these questions, and indeed be encouraged to do so, even though there are no easy answers. Carla van Raay has written of the sexual abuse she suffered at the hands of her father, who instructed her never to disclose the abuse to her priest. She movingly writes:

> I understood quite well that I was not to talk to the priest. I was a bad girl who could not be forgiven. All I could do was to cover up my badness from all the people around me. Even if I succeeded in convincing people I was all right, I couldn't win in the end because God knew my blackness.[5]

It is important not to ignore these cries for help because much can be done to assist in the process of spiritual recovery.

Additionally, it is well documented[6] that being sexually abused in childhood can impact on a survivor's image of God, with God being perceived by the client as 'cruel', 'harsh', 'uncaring' or 'punishing' in the light of the abuse. This results in survivors being more likely to feel uncared for and unloved by God, often perceiving Him to be distant and angry at them over the abuse, and yet longing for a closer relationship with Him. In many ways, the dynamic we referred to earlier in the chapter, where a client longs for connection and yet deeply fears rejection by others, can be seen to be played out in the client's relationship with God. For survivors abused by someone who held a position of responsibility in the Church (eg a priest), the effects can be multiplied, with Christian survivors frequently showing low levels of trust, both in the Church and in aspects of their faith.[7]

The first aim in assisting in this area is, once again, to listen, listen and listen some more. The last thing we want to do, as counsellors or carers, is to give glib answers that appear to 'spiritualise' or gloss over the difficulties. Neither should we attempt answers that are more to do, perhaps, with our own spiritual discomfort about what the survivor is saying than with assisting them to freely express and explore the concerns and questions they have about their spiritual life and faith.

One of the most privileged aspects of work a counsellor might do with a client is to help them in their relationship with God: to rediscover, or perhaps even discover for the first time, that God loves them and was indeed angry, not with them, but over the abuse they suffered in childhood. This may involve gentle reassurance that God *was* not and *is* not distant; that He does *not* see them as worthless or their pain as 'nothing'; that they are *not* who the abuser may have said they are, but *a beloved child of God*.

As we journey with the client, as counsellor or carer, it may be valuable to encourage him/her to write 'an angry psalm': words which can further open up the communication between the survivor and their God. Many of us need to hear that it is not wrong to be angry with God! At least we are communicating!

Research has consistently shown that helping a Christian client to develop a deeper spiritual connection with God can be a valuable part of the recovery process. And, for those who can, establishing such a loving and emotionally connected relationship may give a sense of self-acceptance and belonging, as well as being a source of great emotional comfort.[8]

Christian carers and counsellors, meanwhile, need to remember that their role is to offer the love, care and compassion of Jesus: non-judgmental, patient and accepting. Any theological discussion in the context of counselling is likely to fall flat on its face and render itself counterproductive: and rightly so, for this is not its place. However, as has been said, it can sometimes be helpful to gently offer 'evidence' that however it may seem and 'feel', God is not and was not indifferent to suffering. Care needs to be taken in this area: simply offering a methodical list of 'what we know about God' is unlikely to be helpful. Indeed, if done insensitively, it can leave the client feeling misunderstood and judged. At worst, it can make the client feel that the old and frighteningly familiar abusive patterns are being re-enacted.[9]

Scripture should be used with *very great care* and wisdom. But, bearing in mind that we have already established the value of helping a survivor discover or rediscover God's love, sensitive use of Bible passages (with the client's agreement) can offer a beneficial way to explore and strengthen their beliefs. For example, if the client perceives that God is angry with him/her and not the abuser, it may be helpful to question how that fits with God's 'people priorities' in the Bible: the poor, the weak, the powerless, the forgotten and the marginalised (Isa. 58; Luke 4 and elsewhere); and the fact that God is angry at the abuse done to vulnerable children and adults (Matt. 18:6).

If the client struggles with a belief that God does not care about their suffering, the counsellor may wish to hold that belief up and ask them what they feel about this in the light of the God portrayed biblically as the binder of wounds (Psa. 147:3), the God who is the angry bringer of justice (Psa. 103:6) and the One who weeps for His children. This might be of value in reassuring the client that God cares for them. This same God is the One who is so heartbroken by all that is happening to them that He sends Himself in the form of His Son to intervene and to suffer for them, as one of His children, that they might have life (John 6:40), hope (Titus 2:13) and peace (Eph. 2:14).

NOTE: We must reiterate that we are *not* suggesting that the above or any and every relevant Bible verse should be rolled out in 'evidence' before a client! But if we can help the client verbalise their pain and begin to understand God in terms of a God of love, emotion and story – One who is self-giving and not a static, unmoved figure or indifferent image – we might allow Him to work in this present reality. And if we offer, gradually, a moving, loving narrative of an involved God who cares, works, sweats and weeps for His creation over successive generations, we might help (with the assistance of the Holy Spirit) to release the client from the idea of God being indifferent or distant. This might, in turn, encourage the gradual understanding that God is actually bigger, stronger, higher and deeper than anything or anyone we can know, imagine or experience. Healing may lie in starting to move towards the beginnings of a right, if inevitably incomplete, understanding of just who God is and what He can be to us.

Phillipa wanted to become a Christian. She identified with the Person of Jesus and, being particularly musical and artistic, she responded to the concept of a creator God: it was her love of music and the natural world that had prompted her to ask questions about the nature of life, God and faith in the first place. But she struggled with the idea of God as Father, because her own father had subjected both herself and her two sisters to sexual abuse, early in childhood. Phillipa spent several months with a patient and understanding counsellor who used Phillipa's love of art and music as she helped her to build a clearer, more authentic picture both of what earthly fatherhood was designed to be and what the image of a heavenly Father could mean, particularly in addressing the abuse she had suffered.

Lastly, one way that carers and counsellors might help a client is to ask: 'As we are exploring the abuse, with you standing here and your abuser standing over there, where do you feel God might be standing?' It is likely that God is viewed as an authority figure: the abuse was carried out in the context of authority and power, so authority figures are often emotionally experienced as being on the side of the abuser. Indeed, it is usual for the client engaged in this exercise to instinctively place God on the side of the abuser. By gently questioning this move and asking the client whether they think God would *really* be standing there, given all that they know about Him, assumptions can be brought to the surface which help question the possibly unconscious and unhelpful perceptions of God that the client might hold.

This is complex stuff, fraught with difficulty and bordering on apologetics! And there are, of course, even more complex questions about where God stands in relation to the abuser: questions we probably can't (and perhaps shouldn't attempt to) answer and we must be honest about that. It is our love and concern that should be paramount, not our ability to produce 'evidence' and 'convince'. It is perhaps enough to know that sharing the 'Why?' is often more helpful than offering its answer.

REFLECTION

Read Isaiah 58:6–12.

Isaiah was undoubtedly talking about broad issues of social justice in this stirring prophecy about the 'right' kind of fasting. But these words about the needs of a community are words about our response to individuals: 'chains of injustice'; 'cords of the yoke'; 'oppression'; 'repairing' and 'refreshing' are all words that we might apply to the painful and necessary work with the survivors of abuse.

Often, as Christians in the course of such work, we forget that we are doing God's work and that He blesses us in it.

Read again the words of verses 8–12.

How might these words encourage us as helpers and counsellors as we seek to help others? How might we carry them into our work, silently and humbly, to draw the Holy Spirit into all we do?

PRAYER

God of justice and restoration,
make me Your hands and feet;
Your listening ear and breaking heart;
Your binder of wounds and bringer of hope.
Give me the heart of a servant, on behalf of the Great Healer.
Amen.

CHAPTER 7

WHAT CAN THE CHURCH DO? THE CHRISTIAN RESPONSE TO SURVIVORS OF SEXUAL ABUSE

In this final chapter we consider what the broader Christian response to the survivors of sexual abuse is, and might be, both for the individual in a therapeutic relationship and for the Church. We begin by looking at the issue of forgiveness.

FORGIVENESS AND THE CHURCH

We are considering the issue of forgiveness in this context for two reasons. Firstly, forgiving may be something that a Christian survivor has been 'told' to 'do' by others in church. Secondly, people in the church may have very strong feelings surrounding the need for the survivor to forgive their abuser. This often includes the belief that if they don't forgive, the survivor will in some way 'cut themselves off' from God in their unforgiveness. This illustrates (and may reinforce) some of the difficulties the survivor may experience in their relationship with God, as discussed in the last chapter.

It is fitting that we are considering this issue in the very last chapter because generally (although there are exceptions to every rule) survivors are only in a position to even *begin* to consider the issue of forgiveness, once they have been able to express their pain, their anger and their righteous outrage over the abuse they have endured. Christians in the church can be so anxious to rush the survivor towards forgiving the abuser that they don't give sufficient thought to the injustice and abuse done to the survivor, or to the fact that God is angry at the abuse done to vulnerable children, is the binder of wounds (Psa. 147:3) and the bringer of justice (Psa. 103:6).

So, firstly, we need to recognise that forgiveness is also a journey; something that is to be embarked upon only when the survivor is ready to talk to God about letting go of the injustice and leaving it in His hands.

However, while contemplating forgiveness may take time and be an incredibly difficult issue for a survivor, we cannot, ultimately, escape the fact that forgiveness *is* at the very heart of the gospel.

We are asked to forgive because we have been forgiven by God (Eph. 4:32) and in obedience to God (Matt. 6:14–15; Rom. 12:18). The Bible teaches that forgiveness gives us peace and control over our pain (Gen. 45:1–15; 50:15–21); it also helps us not to become bitter or to carry that bitterness into other areas of our lives. God's love is primarily a reconciling and forgiving love.

But it also asks that the wrongdoer recognise their wrongdoing and be brought to account. Justice and mercy go together (Micah 6:8).

While refusing to forgive someone who is genuinely sorry and repentant is undoubtedly not the example that Jesus gives us, it is wrong to expect survivors of abuse to forgive without any attempt to bring the wrongdoer to account. Left unaccountable they may offend again, causing untold damage in the lives of other innocent victims (something that has all too often been publicised in recent years). So, where it is possible, the abuser needs to be made aware of his or her behaviour and its effects, and understand what caused it (without denial).

Sadly, perpetrators of abuse often don't admit their wrongdoing, leaving clients with a strong sense of injustice and unfinished business. Clients then find it much harder to move on. In addition, of course, an abuser may have died or his/her whereabouts be unknown, making the whole process of forgiveness immensely difficult. Suggesting (however this might be done) that a survivor is less of a person because they cannot forgive at this moment in time risks perpetuating the abuse, albeit in a different form.

We must also remember that forgiveness is a complex process. It involves a decision ('I want to forgive') followed by an ongoing activity (learning to forgive). Sometimes a client does not *want* to forgive – and perhaps never will forgive completely. Very often, the first part of this process starts even further back: a client may need to reach the starting point of wanting just to be *able* to forgive.

Some clients may carry the expectation that, because of their religious beliefs and the biblical basis mentioned earlier, forgiveness must happen before they can recover. So it can be helpful for them to be reassured that they need time – a great deal of time – to express their grief, anger, pain and sorrow at what has happened. Not to take time to do so could cause greater long-term damage.

It may help them to grasp the fact that God is angry at their abuse too. It is also worth highlighting to them the often missed fact that even Jesus did not *Himself* forgive *His* offenders initially, but instead asked God to do so.

We also need to distinguish between forgiving and forgetting. These two are often married one to the other in popular perception, but even when forgiveness might be thinkable and do-able, forgetting should *not* be considered something that the survivor must achieve. Neither does forgiveness for abuse mean that what happened was 'all right'; nor that 'it matters less now'. Forgiveness which implies that the abuser's actions were, in some way, justified is not healthy forgiveness. It *did* happen and it was *not* 'all right' and it will *never* 'matter less'. What the abuser did will never be acceptable, either to the abused, to society or to God.

In summary, forgiveness is never about letting someone 'off the hook'. To introduce the subject of forgiveness could be interpreted, in the extreme, as saying: 'I've heard all you're saying, but now it's time to let the abuser off because it didn't really matter that much.' Nevertheless, forgiveness *is* ultimately beneficial to a survivor, because it is largely about letting go of self-destructive anger. For a Christian wanting to be able to forgive, it is powerful and therapeutic for them to be able to come to a place where they are willing and able (both mentally and emotionally) to place the abuser into the hands of God – to let God decide what justice is to be done.

(The subject of forgiveness is explored in a companion Insight Guide.)

PRACTICAL IMPLICATIONS FOR PRAYER MINISTRY

The history of our 'dealing with' or 'handling' victims of abuse, either as individuals or as church communities, is not always a history to be proud of – largely because we use those particular verbs! Much of what mars that history comes out of shock, embarrassment, misunderstanding or ignorance; or a desire to 'fix it' or to 'overspiritualise' human pain and suffering. This is not least the case in terms of prayer ministry and approaches to healing. That both are important and often effective is not in doubt. But we must always remember that prayer is a privilege and that healing is a gift. We should never impose prayer or healing practices, including so-called 'deliverance', on those whose very fear is embedded in acts of misused authority, secretive behaviour and unwanted ritual and physical touching: the innocent laying on of hands for blessing can replicate abuse in the mind of the client.

Sometimes just praying for the person and saying nothing can be the wisest course of action. There is no substitute for care and love, based on well-informed skill and experience and genuine empathy.

Diana had been taught by her abuser that the abuse was God punishing her for being naughty. This experience instilled a deep hatred of any notion of God or of any kind of 'religious person'. The abuse itself almost became buried beneath Diana's hatred. When Diana went to university she made friends with two girls in her hall that she later discovered were Christians. Diana immediately began to behave extremely negatively towards them. Bewildered and hurt, they sought to discover the source of Diana's obvious vitriol – and eventually she told them. They decided not to engage in debate, nor to go out of their way to 'set the record straight', sensing that God was bigger than anything they might say or do. Instead, they did not give up on her. Together they prayed for her, and continued to invite her to join their activities. Almost despite herself, and because the two girls were friendly and fun, Diana joined in. For the whole of their three years together, the group shared lots of fun and laughter – and the occasional, increasingly light-hearted, argument about 'their God'. Their love and authenticity of faith made an impact on Diana and, after three and a half years, she began to show a genuine interest in their faith. They had done nothing but be there for the long haul and had 'loved and let God'.

PRACTICAL IMPLICATIONS FOR SAFEGUARDING CHILDREN

The Government has defined the term 'safeguarding children' as follows:

The process of protecting children from abuse and neglect, preventing impairment of their health and development and ensuring they are growing up in circumstances consistent with the provision of safe and effective care that enables children to have optimum life chances and enter adulthood successfully.[2]

Having reached an understanding of the devastating effects of abuse, we need to take the aforementioned definition seriously. Indeed, we cannot stress strongly enough that churches, schools, youth clubs and para-church organisations should establish wise, informed, workable safeguarding policies, ensuring that the children are at all times protected when under their care. Leadership teams should be fully conversant with both correct policy and right practice, not just in terms of what is to be done, or not done, but why. At all times we need to remember: the welfare of a child is paramount.

PRACTICAL IMPLICATIONS FOR CHURCH AND WORSHIP

There is an oft-missed extension to these issues for church and worship leaders. If we are to welcome and care for survivors of abuse within our worshipping communities, we need to be, quietly and unobtrusively, aware of ways in which practices, which are very familiar and comfortable to us, may be far from either for survivors of abuse. We do this, not by flagging up such issues publicly so that clients feel the spotlight turned upon them as a 'special case', nor in ways which overlook or complicate the needs of others in the church. Rather we must think carefully about things we do which might make it more difficult for a survivor to make progress within a community which seeks to love and support them as a whole person – and, most particularly, as a person who wishes to grow closer to God and other people, as a part of that community.

We might ask ourselves:
- Have worship leaders been asked to consider some of the things they do and say which might prove difficult for survivors of abuse? For example: 'Why not give someone near you a GREAT BIG hug this morning!'

- Does 'shove up in the pew' or 'get into a holy huddle' mean too much physical closeness for some people to be able cope with? Could single, well-spaced chairs be available too?

- Have we considered some of the language we use in liturgy and worship and the connotations it might have? Has it become so familiar that it would benefit from explanation occasionally? (For example, 'washed by the blood of sacrifice' is a pretty scary concept, at the best of times!)

- During communion, are there ways to offer survivors (and everyone) the opportunity to take bread and wine for themselves rather than be given it direct to their mouths/lips?

- Do we almost 'insist' on closing eyes, sitting or standing, at certain points? Do our directions sometimes sound like orders, coercion, appeal or persuasion? How often do we explain the meaning and purpose of symbols and ritual – for *everyone's* benefit?

In general terms:
- Do we maintain general guidelines about physical safety and boundaries in pastoral situations, especially – but not only – where male–female relationships and co-working is concerned?

And lastly,
- Do we *really* foster and encourage, even directly teach, genuine love and acceptance of *every* person who joins our worshipping community, whatever their life experience, history, handicap

or behaviour? (It's a sad fact that many clients of sexual abuse suffer almost as much from how others respond, or how they fear they might respond to their abuse, as from their memories.)

Whilst we can't become oversensitive or neurotic about these issues and will never be able to protect survivors from every element they might find difficult, simple measures can be taken to make their experience of church and worship a less threatening or isolating one.

Mary, an older church member, was slowly recovering, with the help of her counsellor, from long-held memories of sexual abuse. Although she did not blame God, she had always (and still) struggled with the close physical proximity of other people – especially men and, as she put it, 'their smells'. When the weather was warm or a man wore aftershave, she would inwardly panic and often begin to feel physically sick, even many, many years after the abuse. Mary could work through her anxiety and fear using her relaxation techniques, if she had physical space and an exit route in the church or church hall. So, together with her counsellor and the vicar, it was arranged that a couple of seats would always be casually and as unobtrusively as possible 'reserved' for Mary close to the door – usually with a red jumper and a bag! Everyone soon assumed that Mary became dizzy in hot and close places, a myth that all concerned were happy to perpetuate until Mary felt more able to cope.

CONTINUING THE JOURNEY BEYOND ABUSE

We have spoken of the need for mercy and justice to go hand in hand on this journey; of the difficulty of the landscape of forgiveness; and of the hope of healing and wholeness. The relationship between these elements is a difficult one, involving tentative steps both forward and back. While healing is an internal process, often slow and faltering, never easy, never free of scars, justice is external and often beyond the control of either client or supporter. Yet as Chevous,[3] quoted in 'Responding Well', writes:

> Healing and justice are bound up with continuing transformation of the lives of those who have experienced abuse, so that they are more likely to recover and flourish. Healing is a journey towards wholeness, whereby clients may move from being victims less often and clients or 'thrivers' in more of their lives.

It is our role, as accompaniers on that journey, to go the distance and to do all we can to assist that transformation.

REFLECTION

Look back over some of the Gospel accounts of Jesus' responses that you read earlier. Spend time reflecting generally upon them. Think about how and why they might particularly speak to you.

Jesus was remarkable, stunning, often shocking, not least in His acceptance of, and relationships with, those who were marked (or marked themselves) as valueless, weak or somehow 'unclean': the outsider, the leper, the tax collector, the adulteress, the Samaritan woman. He was the 'safe place' for their pain. It was with Jesus that they felt heard, knew genuine compassion and sympathy and, most importantly, were offered a way to move beyond their pain and suffering.

As we have discussed, survivors of abuse falsely, but understandably, may very well see themselves as of less value, as unclean, as outsiders. But in every word and action Jesus says: *This is not so.* Instead He says those who believe they are the least will be first; those who are weakest are strongest; those who have nothing will have everything. He imparts value and worth, offering love and eternal hope beyond imagining to those who feel anything but lovable and hopeful.

So what does that mean for us? Well, it's our brief as we continue His work, isn't it?

Our brief to offer a safe place, to listen, to give value and worth and to show a way beyond the pain and suffering of abuse: to restore the self-image of the man or woman who is wonderfully made in God's image.

If we do nothing else as individuals, as churches, as part of humanity, we can share one another's suffering on the journey: it's what Jesus did to the utmost. As we do so, we will perhaps make the road ahead for all who suffer, however shadowed, one of compassion, love and hope ...

PRAYER

Gracious, loving and forgiving God,

We ask for Your very real presence in the midst of our conversations,

That the true and loving Father of the greatest story will redeem stories of pain;

That the Son who knows suffering and scars will share our tears;

That the Holy Spirit, the Counsellor, will be our inspiration, our wisdom and our guide, as we accompany Your wholly and amazingly loved ones on a journey of hope.
Amen.

PRACTICAL GUIDELINES FOR PASTORAL CARE

Carers should be aware of the following:

- As soon as they become involved in any form of pastoral care they will inevitably be faced with survivors who have been sexually abused in childhood.

- Abusers come from every social background, religion, employment and ethnic background. It is *impossible* to identify who might be, or *who might become*, an abuser. Therefore we cannot stress strongly enough the importance of ensuring that a church or organisation has a robust and effective safeguarding policy. This will mean that all church workers in contact with children undertake a CRB check and are given training about avoiding situations where they are alone with children.

- When talking to someone who has been abused, it is of paramount importance to be sensitive and to give them the freedom and permission to talk about what has happened. Any response should be helpful, gentle, sensitive and empathic, without any hint of blame for the abuse, and it should reinforce the message that it was *not their fault*; that a child wasn't and never is to blame for childhood sexual abuse.

- A survivor may be reluctant to talk about the abuse for a number of reasons: for example, a fear of rejection, a fear of being labelled a potential abuser, a wish to avoid the memory, a wish to protect the abuser etc.

- The carer must not be afraid to seek professional help. (See contact details which follow.)

- Special sensitivity is needed around the issue of touch. It is probably better not to touch unless the abused person asks for a touch or hug – and even then with 'hidden' caution, to avoid misinterpretation.

- Supporting a survivor, showing them love and compassion, is the most helpful and powerful thing a carer can offer. The power of listening and believing the survivor cannot be overestimated in bringing healing and wholeness.

- For Christians, sexual abuse in childhood can have a devastating effect on how they believe God views them. A survivor is to be reminded that God sees them as His precious child, dearly loved. (Nevertheless, listen first and give advice and reminders later.)

- Very careful thought is needed as to what is meant by forgiveness. Forgiveness does not mean that the abuse did not matter, nor that it is acceptable. The survivor may need frequent reminders that abuse is never acceptable to God and that He is angry with those who impart injustice and suffering.

- Keeping confidentiality is vital. Trust is a huge issue for survivors. Carers should not break or damage the trust the survivor has placed in them.

- Self-care is essential, seeking supervisory support if possible, whilst respecting the boundaries of confidentiality.

USEFUL CONTACTS

Association of Christian Counsellors
ACC, 29 Momus Boulevard, Coventry, CV2 5NA
Tel: 0845 124 9569 Website: www.acc-uk.org

British Association for Counselling and Psychotherapy
BACP, BACP House, 15 St John's Business Park, Lutterworth, Leicestershire, LE17 4HB
Tel: 01455 883300 (Customer Services); Fax: 01455 550243
Website: www.bacp.co.uk

NSPCC National Society for the Prevention of Cruelty to Children
Child Protection Helpline, P.O. Box 18222, London, EC2A 3RU
Tel: 0808 800 5000 Website: www.nspcc.org.uk

Childline
(For a child to talk in confidence to a counsellor/adult)
Tel: 0800 1111

Churches Child Protection Advisory Service
PCCA Christian Child Care, P.O. Box 133, Swanley, Kent, BR8 7UQ Tel: 01322 660011

NOTES

CHAPTER 1

1. P. Easteal, *Survivors of sexual assault: A National Survey.* Available online at http:www.aic.gov.au/publications/proceedings (1992). See also J.M. Flemming, 'Prevalence of Childhood Sexual Abuse in a Community Example of Australian Women', *Medical Journal of Australia*, Vol. 166, No. 2, 1997, pp.65-68.
2. Marie Fortune, *Clergy Misconduct: Sexual Abuse in the Ministerial Relationship* (Seattle: Faith Trust Institute, 2009).
3. J.P. Wilson and R.B. Thomas, *Empathy in the Treatment of Trauma and PTSD* (New York: Brunner Routledge, 2004).
4. Information Sharing: Guidance for Practitioners and Managers 008, Para. 340, p.21. Department of Education: www. education.gov.uk

CHAPTER 2

1. American National Center on Child Abuse and Neglect, *Sexual Abuse – Child Abuse: An Overview.* www.findcounselling.com/journal/childabuse/sexualabuse.html (1978).
2. *Working Together to Safeguard Children* www.education.gov.uk/publications??eOrderingDownload?00305-2010DOM-EN.PDF (2010) p.38.
3. www.stopthetraffik.org
4. *Working Together to Safeguard Children*, ibid. (2010), www.education.gov.uk/publications
5. P. Cawson et al., *Child Maltreatment in the United Kingdom: A Study of the Prevalence of Child Abuse and Neglect* (London: NSP.CC, 2000).
6. Lucy Faithfull Foundation Child Protection Charity: www.lucyfaithfull.org

7. N. Richardson and L. Broomfield, *Who Abuses Children?* National Child Protection Clearing House, Australian Institute of Family Studies, Melbourne (2005).
8. Childline case notes: NSPCC, http://www.nspcc.org.uk/inform/publications/case notes
9. Cawson et al., ibid.
10. Home Office Research, Development and Statistics Directorate, March 2004.
11. David Fergusson and Paul Mullen, *Childhood Sexual Abuse: An Evidence-Based Perspective* (London: Sage, 1999). See also J.E. Taylor and S. Harvey, 'A meta-analysis of the effects of psychotherapy with adults sexually abused in childhood', *Clinical Psychology Review*, Vol. 30, 2010, pp.749–767.
12. See Mary Berry, 'Sexual abuse in childhood', in Colin Feltham and Ian Horton (eds), *Handbook of Counselling and Psychotherapy* (London: Sage Publications, 2000).
13. E. Bass and L. Davis, *The Courage to Heal: A Guide for Women Survivors of Child Sexual Abuse* (New York: Harper and Row, 1988).
14. D.A. Bekerian and S.J. Goodrich, 'Recovered Memories of Child Sexual Abuse', in G.E. Berrios and J.R. Hodges (eds), *Memory Disorders in Psychiatric Practice* (Cambridge: Cambridge University Press, 2000).
15. Charles S. Carver and Michael F. Scheier, *Perspectives on Personality* (London: Allyn and Bacon, 2000).

CHAPTER 3

1. P. McClendon, *Incest/Sexual abuse of children*, American Academy of Experts in Traumatic Stress, http:/www.aaets.org/article121.htm
2. Anne Lazenbatt, The Impact of abuse and neglect on the health and mental health of young people. NSPCC: www.nspcc.org.uk 2010.
3. 'Responding Well to Sexual Abuse', The Church of England, 2011, p.19.
4. John Bowlby, *Attachment and Loss: Separation, Anger and Anxiety*, Vol. 2 (London: Hogarth Press, 1973).
5. David J. Wallin, *Attachment in Psychotherapy* (New York: Guilford Publications Ltd, 2007).

6. M. Main and J. Solomon, 'Discovery of an insecure disorganized/ disoriented attachment pattern: procedures, findings and implications for the classification of behavior', in T. Braxelton and M. Yogman (eds), *Affective Development in Infancy* (Norwood, NJ: Ablex, 1986), pp.95-124.
7. G. Liotti, 'Trauma, Dissociation and Disorganised Attachment: Three strands of a single braid', in *Psychotherapy, Research, Practice and Training*, 2004, Vol. 41, pp.472-486.
8. Sue Gerhardt, *Why Love Matters* (Hove: Brunner-Routledge, 2004).
9. See also J.E. Taylor, and S. Harvey, 'A meta-analysis of the effects of psychotherapy with adults sexually abused in childhood', *Clinical Psychology Review*, Vol. 30, 2010, pp.749-767.
10. B. Van der Kolk, A. McFarlane and L. Weisaeth (eds), *Traumatic Stress: The Effects of Overwhelming Experience on Mind, Body and Society* (New York: Guilford Press, 1996).
11. See *American Journal of Psychiatry*, Vol. 152, No. 9, 1995.
12. C.S. Widom, Cathy, S., and Susanne Hiller-Sturmhöfel, 'Alcohol abuse as a risk factor for and consequence of child abuse', *Journal of Substance Abuse*, Vol. 11, (1), 2000.

CHAPTER 4
1. S.E. Ullman, 'Social Reactions to Child Abuse Disclosures: A Critical Review', *Journal of Child Sexual Abuse*, Vol. 12, Issue 1, 2003, pp. 88-121, as cited in 'Responding Well to Sexual Abuse', ibid.

CHAPTER 5
1. J.E. Taylor and S. Harvey, 'A meta-analysis of the effects of psychotherapy with adults sexually abused in childhood', *Clinical Psychology Review*, Vol. 30, 2010, pp.749-767.
2. Yvonne Dolan, *Beyond Survival: Living Well is the Best Revenge* (London: BT Press, 2000, 2nd edit.).
3. Frederick Buechner, *Beyond Words: Daily Readings in the ABC's of Faith* (New York: Harper Collins, 2004).

CHAPTER 6

1. Julianne Holt-Lunstead, Timothy B. Smith and J. Bradley Layton, 'Social Relationships and Mortality Risk: A Meta Analytic Review', www.plosmedicine.org Vol. 10, issue 7, 2010.
2. Julianne Holt-Lunstead, T.B. Smith and J.B. Layton, ibid.
3. Chris Ledger and Wendy Bray, *Insight into Self-Esteem* (Farnham, UK: CWR, 2006).
4. N.A. Murray-Swank and K. Pargament, 'God, where are you? Evaluating a spiritually integrated intervention for sexual abuse', in *Mental Health, Religion and Culture*, Vol. 8 (3), pp.191-203.
5. Carla van Raay, *God's Callgirl: A Memoir* (Sydney: Harper Collins, 2004), as cited by B. Crisp, (2007) *Spirituality and Sexual Abuse, Theology and Sexuality*, 13 (3), (2005) pp.301-314.
6. T.L. Gall et al., 'Spirituality and the Current Adjustment of Adult Survivors of Childhood Sexual Abuse', *Journal for the Scientific Study of Religion*, Vol. 46 (1), 2007, pp.101-117.
7. S.J. Rossetti, 'Impact of Child Sexual Abuse on Attitudes Toward God and the Catholic Church', *Child Abuse and Neglect*, Vol. 19 (12), 1995, pp.1469-1481, as cited by T.L. Gall et al., 'Spirituality and the Current Adjustment of Adult Survivors of Childhood Sexual Abuse', *Journal for the Scientific Study of Religion*, Vol. 46 (1), 2007, pp.101-117.
8. Ibid. See also W.C. Rowatt and L.A. Kirkpatrick, 'Two Dimensions of Attachment to God and their Relation to Affect, Religiosity, and Personality Constructs', *Journal for the Scientific Study of Religion*, Vol. 41 (4), 2002, pp.637-651.
9. P. Fouque and Martin Glachan, 'The impact of Christian counselling on clients of sexual abuse', *Counselling Psychology Quarterly*, Vol. 13 (2), 2000, pp.201-220.

CHAPTER 7

1. Ron Kallmier and Sheila Jacobs, *Insight into Forgiveness* (Farnham, UK: CWR, 2008).
2. www.safeguardingchildren.org
3. J. Chevous, *From Silence to Sanctuary: A Guide to Understanding, Preventing and Responding to Abuse* (London: SPCK, 2005).

Courses and seminars

Publishing and new media

Conference facilities

Transforming lives

CWR's vision is to enable people to experience personal transformation through applying God's Word to their lives and relationships.

Our Bible-based training and resources help people around the world to:
• Grow in their walk with God
• Understand and apply Scripture to their lives
• Resource themselves and their church
• Develop pastoral care and counselling skills
• Train for leadership
• Strengthen relationships, marriage and family life and much more.

Our insightful writers provide daily Bible-reading notes and other resources for all ages, and our experienced course designers and presenters have gained an international reputation for excellence and effectiveness.

CWR's Training and Conference Centre in Surrey, England, provides excellent facilities in an idyllic setting – ideal for both learning and spiritual refreshment.

CWR Applying God's Word
to everyday life and relationships

CWR, Waverley Abbey House,
Waverley Lane, Farnham,
Surrey GU9 8EP, UK

Telephone: +44 (0)1252 784700
Email: info@cwr.org.uk
Website: www.cwr.org.uk

Registered Charity No 294387
Company Registration No 1990308